DISCOVER THE PROCESS COMMUNICATION MODEL®

DISCOVER THE PROCESS COMMUNICATION MODEL®

Jerome Lefeuvre

Copyright © 2017 by Jerome Lefeuvre.

Library of Congress Control Number:	2017906126
ISBN: Hardcover	978-1-5434-1732-6
Softcover	978-1-5434-1731-9
eBook	978-1-5434-1730-2

All rights reserved. No part of this book may be reproduced or transmitted in any form or by any means, electronic or mechanical, including photocopying, recording, or by any information storage and retrieval system, without permission in writing from the copyright owner.

Print information available on the last page.

Rev. date: 06/22/2017

To order additional copies of this book, contact:
Xlibris
1-888-795-4274
www.Xlibris.com
Orders@Xlibris.com
758343

Contents

Introduction ix

Chapter 1: A Little History... 1

Chapter 2: Principles and Applications of the Process
Communication Model 9

Chapter 3: The Process Communication Model and the Six
Personality Types 30

Chapter 4: The Essential Components of the Personality
Structure 52

Chapter 5: FAQs about The Process Communication Model 81

Appendix 85

Selected bibliography 103

To know more 113

KCI Copyrighted Elements 115

PROCESS COMMUNICATION MODEL®
Kahler Communications, Inc.

Introduction

What is the Process Communication Model®?

The Process Communication Model® (PCM) is a methodology for the discovery and understanding of one's own personality as well as those of others. It rests on two basic concepts:

1. *How things are said is as important and often more important, than what is said.* The other person reacts, for better or for worse, to the music behind the words, known as "Process." In a daily management context the repeated bombardment of "miscommunication" may lead to de-motivation, loss of creativity, and counter-productivity; "What's the use?" and "He/she doesn't understand" are indications that we were unable, in that situation, to communicate with the other person, that is to say to transmit *clear messages* and/or to *listen*.

A good communication process enables the optimization of the relationship by going directly to the essentials and to build using the best in each of us. Conversely, an incompatible process runs the risk of creating "a missed communication," a source, at first, of misunderstanding and possibly a total lack of understanding leading to conflict.

> 2   *There are six basic Personality Types, and during our lives to some degree, we each develop characteristics of all of them.* We all have a *basic Personality Type* or *Base*, acquired for life, and a *Phase type* -sometimes the same type as our Base- that determines our sources of psychological motivation. Additionally these types also indicate our most probable reactions when we are showing signs of stress. We all have these six Personality Types in common. What separates us is the order of preference we give to them and our own personal way of maintaining and developing them.

> Understanding these six typologies provides the keys required to understand and nourish our own personal needs and thus enables us to adapt our communications strategies, to react appropriately to the needs of those around us, and to build constructive and efficient relationships in both the short and the long term. These healthy communication strategies can be developed.

1.   "Process communication": what is it for?

Each Personality Type has its codes, language, and its own "frame of reference". Each Personality Type sends out unique signals when entering into stress that can cause miscommunication.

Research shows that 93% of the spoken message is encoded in non-verbal signals: voice-tones, postures, gestures and facial expressions. Only 7% of the message is conveyed through the words. (Mehrabian and Ferris 1967) This emphasizes the interest and importance of understanding the codes and signals emitted by both sides of the communication equation, self and other.

In the Process Communication Model, we place the emphasis upon *how to say it*, rather than on *what to say*. Process rather than content.

> The Process Communication Model serves to initiate communication with others by being in tune not only with what they say, but also with what they feel and believe.

Understanding personality provides the keys to develop well-tuned communication strategies, to react in appropriate ways to the demands of one's associates and friends, and in turn to build quickly, constructive and effective relationships. These multiple applications of the Process Communication Model are recognized in the professional world of companies, the behavioral and emotional development of individuals, and therapy.

> ### The Process Communication Model
> #### some numbers
>
> Over a million people worldwide have profitably used this model in one way or another.
> Since 1992, over 1,110,000 profiles have been established using the Process Communication Model questionnaire, of which over 17,000 were in a single clinical field; 60,000 profiles in 2016 alone.
> People in 42 countries on five continents have directly requested profiles. More than 2400 trainers, coaches and recruiters have been certified in the world.

# Chapter 1

A Little History…

"If you want them to listen to what you say, talk their language…"
Taibi Kahler

1. How it all began…

In 1971 Dr. Taibi Kahler observed that his patients communicated with others, positively or negatively, using identifiable, repetitive sequences.

What was new in his approach was that he recognized that by second-by-second observation of an individual, during any communication, it was possible to quantify the time spent in positive and negative communication. With his methods it was quite simple to establish predictable patterns of how each Personality Type communicated, as observed behaviors were *sequential, measurable*, and *predictable*.

Taibi Kahler then went on to correlate his observations into six personality typologies that he called miniscripts. For this pioneering work, he was awarded the prestigious Eric Berne Memorial Scientific Award.

In 1982 the definitive, validated, and proven Process Communication Model took flight.

2. Influences and Helping Hands

It would be over-simplifying to think that the Process Communication Model is born only from Taibi Kahler's research into predictable behavior in humans. It is rather a meeting of several influences that led to the discovery of the six Personality Types and the methods that have arisen from this discovery.

2.1 The Work of Eric Berne on Transactional Analysis and Life Scripts

The most evident and most important influence is that born from the inspirational work of Dr. Eric Berne, Taibi Kahler's mentor, on the Transactional Analysis of life scripts.

In mid-1950 Eric Berne, a classically trained psychiatrist and analyst, observed that none of the heroic figures or divinities in Greek mythology had happy destinies.

Eric Berne with his brilliant Cartesian mind, didn't stop there; he decided to learn Greek to be able to read these texts in the original language. His laudable effort enabled him to verify that, indeed, in these ancient texts, not one hero or god of Greek mythology had a happy end. On the contrary, they all finished in the abyss of malediction or had a less-than-enviable fate. This led him intuitively to the conclusion that it is "Human mythology" rather than Greek, Roman or Egyptian, to see the tragedy in life. The ancient authors saw the difficulty of "being," and their texts carried within them all the possible "script scenarios" leading to success or failure.

Our life scripts, as old as mythology!

And what if there were an unconscious transmission of these scripts from mother to son, from father to daughter, from generation to generation, or from civilization to civilization? -- Hercules condemned to accomplish the twelve tasks; Arachne, condemned to weave all her life; Cassandra whose clairvoyance was of no avail...

If the destinies were part of one enormous, collective unconscious, would it explain the fact that in a different century, we are destined to commit the same mistakes as Hercules, Arachne, and the others? And what if that explained why we have this strange tendency to fall into the same traps and make the same mistakes over and over again throughout our lives?

For example, if my script is that of Hercules, it would explain why I have a tendency not to know how to have fun before having completed the tasks at hand perfectly.

If my preferred script is that of Cassandra, it would, perhaps, explain why I regularly find myself "knowing for certain" how things will turn out, while being unable to influence any one to believe me.

Eric Berne's reflections led him to the discovery that each of us has our own "pre-written" script in early childhood before seven years of age, that contains productive beliefs that enable us to succeed and excel, and at the same time, unproductive beliefs that when activated lead us to make bad choices, those that we will often repeat over and over again.

The good news is that if we can recognize or discover our script, we can act on this and avoid the pitfalls.

> **BERNE'S DEFINITION OF LIFE SCRIPT**
>
> An unconscious life plan based on decisions made in childhood, reinforced by parents, justified by subsequent events, leading to a predictable outcome.

Taibi Kahler was soon interested in Berne's practice, and his keen observation of repetitive human behaviors noticed in script theory led to his research and discovery of the Process Communication Model.

Transactional Analysis theories and concepts such as "Ego States" find their echoes in "Personality Parts," while "transactions" led to the discovery of "Communication Channels." The concept "Hungers," such as "need of recognition and time structure," take the form of eight discrete psychological needs, and the concept of "life script," the cornerstone of Berne's work, is found in the six Failure Patterns identified by Taibi Kahler entitled: Always, Never, After, Until, Almost Type 1 and Almost Type 2.

Common mistakes of trainers or consultants in transactional analysis workshops and seminars is to give Eric Berne rather than Taibi Kahler the credit for being the father of the fascinating concept of *behavioral Drivers and Process Scripts Patterns*.

2.2 Adaptations and Personality Types: the Work of Paul Ware

In the 1970's and 1980's, Paul Ware, a psychiatrist, undertook a considerable amount of work on establishing contact with psychotic patients by identifying what he termed "Adaptations."

Starting from the work of Shapiro and following the path traced by Kahler, Ware integrated into his work the psychiatric criteria Diagnostic and Statistical Manual (DSM) and took from Kahler the six Personality Types or Adaptations that he equated with the notion of "disorder."

These "disorders", or dysfunctional adaptations to reality, were called: **Over-reactor, Cycloid, Workaholic, Sceptic, Daydreamer, Critic, and Manipulator**. It is interesting to note that Paul Ware also found six terms relating to the traits of six of the then-recognized Personality Disorders and labeled them: Histrionic, Paranoid, Anti-Social, Obsessive Compulsive, Schizoid and Passive Aggressive.

2.2.1 Doors of Communication

Additionally, Ware suggested the hypothesis that individuals develop specific character traits according to their preferential mode of adaptation to their reality.

It is only when these personality traits are maladaptive and cause significant difficulties or generates distress, that they constitute a personality disorder.

Paul Ware observed that there were three contact zones through which to communicate or to initiate contact with his patients, demonstrating behavioral traits of these "disorders." He called the contact zones, "doors," describing them as follows:

1. The *Open door* represents the way to make effective contact with the patient;
2. The *Target door* represents the point in need of development;
3. The *Trap door* represents the area to avoid as it leads to blocking of the effective exchange between therapist and patient.

He identified the three possible *doors* (or contact zones with an individual) as Thoughts, Feelings and Behaviors.

Using a part of Kahler's work on *behavioral drivers*, Ware provided Process Communication with a perspective of a strong response to the question: How can a positive contact with an individual under stress be re-established?

Kahler was on his way to explain the process at work with these three doors, one to initiate contact, the open door, another to motivate, the target door, and the last to avoid, a trap door. From this starting point, Kahler refined the concept, discovering six means of establishing contact. Kahler called them "contact perceptions."

In 2006, Dr. Paul Ware used the Process Communication Model (PCM) to facilitate effective therapeutic interventions when working with personality disorders. In addition to and beyond his psychiatric work, he developed together with his wife, Dr. Lisa Harper-Ware, an application for family therapy based on PCM. PCM showed itself to be very effective in initiating communication and positive contact between various members of a "family system," enabling numerous individuals to create positive and durable links.

3. NASA Makes Its Contribution

In the 1970's, psychiatrist, Dr. Terry McGuire, who was then employed in the recruitment of flight crews for the United States National Aeronautics and Space Administration (NASA), faced the challenge of recruiting crews for a mission that even today is considered as one of the greatest steps for mankind, the mission of manned flight to the moon.

During a presentation he made at a conference in Paris, this charming and slightly in-the-stars (yes, "Can do!") man told us that the first part of his career was devoted to human resistance to physical and then psychological pain. His often-frightening and sometimes amusing tale explained why, one fine day, tired of seeing suffering and pain, he decided to change direction before his work became unbearable.

In 1978, he heard about a brilliant, young psychologist that claimed to be capable of predicting, after an interview of only a few minutes, whether the stress behavior of an individual in an unpleasant situation would be light or severe. This diagnosis enabled Dr. Kahler, through early identification, to recommend a mode of intervention and training to provide individuals the means to stop the stress process, or in other words, to stop the negative pattern from being worked out....

3.1 Recruiting Astronauts

Terry McGuire invited this young psychologist to participate in a new recruiting campaign for NASA. He was so impressed that he influenced NASA to fund additional research to create a questionnaire to identify the psychological structure of an individual and to develop the observation of new components outside of stress, such as:

- The Dominant Management Style;
- Preferential Environments;
- Communication Channels, and
- The Mode of Language to be Used called Perceptions.

In 1982, the Process Communication Management Model was born. It enabled an organization to offer its staff a communication, motivation, and stress-management model that encompassed the four key domains of emotional intelligence[1]:

- Self-Awareness;
- Social Awareness;
- Self-Management, and
- Relationship Management.

4. Friend of a Future President

In the early 1980's, Taibi Kahler was living in Little Rock, Arkansas. His neighbors were a promising young couple. Bill and Hillary, their first names, were looking for someone to help them deal with a difficult person that was calling regularly and threatening their daughter. Even though Bill Clinton was not yet president, he was an important figure on the political scene and the potential threat could not be taken lightly.

Taibi Kahler, with his reputation as an effective psychologist, was called on to deal with the situation. He took the next threatening call. The caller gave himself up to the police a short time after.

This anecdote explains how the Clintons and Kahler began their long relationship, professional as well as personal.

To what extent the American Administration used PCM is not easy to determine precisely; few sources are authorized to speak out. Let's simply say that for several years, PCM was a daily factor in this major administration and that Bill Clinton would call on Taibi Kahler for advice and counsel throughout his career.

---

[1] Goleman-Boyatsis-McKee

Taibi Kahler: A Short Biography

Dr. Taibi Kahler is today President Emeritus of Kahler Communications Inc., with headquarters in Hot Springs, Arkansas, and offices in major capital cities throughout the world.

Dr. Kahler holds several doctorates in human sciences, in particular in Child Development and Family Life.

He is a clinical psychologist both in the domains of family life and professional environment.

Over one million people, worldwide, have requested a personality profile inventory, the *Process Communication Profile*.

Dr. Kahler was invited by Dr. Terry McGuire, psychiatric consultant to NASA, to participate in the recruitment of astronaut crews.

A member of thirteen American and International organizations, his Intelligence Quotient (IQ) is among the highest on the planet.

Dr. Kahler is a long-time friend of and communications counselor to the former American President, William Jefferson Clinton, and has contributed to the work of the American Administration via his communication and management model (PCM) and his psychotherapy model (*The Process Therapy Model®*).

Chapter 2

Principles and Applications of the Process Communication Model

1. The Process Communication Model mechanism

When two people interact and want to understand each other, they can choose a mode of communication that "fits" with the other. If the mode of communication does indeed suit the other, he/she "hears" correctly what is being said. They are both then able to make decisions together and work effectively. (We often call this being in-tune.) But if the mode of communication does not make an easy fit for the other person, there is a risk of misunderstanding or even worse, no understanding at all.

1.1 To be Understood, One Must Be Heard!

If the resultant misunderstanding in the exchange is not quickly corrected by "shifting" to the style best-suited to the other, the two will move rapidly from misunderstanding to *miscommunication* which can quickly descend into a state of unproductive stress (anxiety or conflict).

Under negative stress we no longer perceive reality accurately; we misinterpret messages from our environment and experience emotions that lead us even deeper into our state of anxiety. At this point we often make inappropriate choices, as well as unhelpful decisions, and we show distress in our behavior.

In these circumstances it may be helpful to advise people in a state of miscommunication not to take any decision that could affect either their relationship or the future of their collaboration.

1.2   How Can Miscommunication Be Avoided?

To avoid misunderstandings leading to Distress and Miscommunications we need to be aware of and use PCM that is to say *use a style of communication selected to fit the communication style of the other person and in this way send messages that will be heard without misinterpretation."*

1.3   How Can the Process Be Used without Making Mistakes?

The first condition is that we, ourselves, need to be in a positive state, that is to say, in-tune with our environment, others and ourselves. Essentially, this means assuming the win/win frame of mind. To be in this positive state, we need to know what our own needs are and how to meet them.

According to Taibi Kahler, there are six different Personality Types each of which has different needs. What we all have in common is the necessity to know what our needs are and how to meet them positively:

If we are unable to achieve this, we may easily enter into stress behaviors or even anxiety as this negatively affects our communication with those around us, in both our professional or personal lives.

If, on the other hand, our needs are positively met, we are capable of communication. We can access the six available Personality Types within ourselves and utilize their specific resources. Thus, we can more easily establish harmonious and effective relationships in both our professional and personal lives.

2. The Fundamental Principles of the Process Communication Model

Below are some of the core beliefs and principles of PCM.

We make no value judgement in this model.

No Personality Type or structure is better than another.

The structure is presented in the form of a six-floor building, each floor representing one Personality Type.

It is possible to structure these six floors in all possible combinations - a total of 720 combinations ("six factorial"). The order of the floors indicates the preferred order of each individual.

Throughout the day we can visit any of the "floors" of our building depending on the demands of our environment.

The higher the floor, the more energy is needed both to reach and to spend time there, and prolonged periods in any relatively infrequently visited floor can lead to negative stress.

To communicate effectively we must be on the "floor" that the other person will best hear.

The Base personality is determined in the first moments of life and never changes.

We "hear" with our Base (the Base language is the clearest, most audible, and most motivating for others to initiate contact with us.) Our capacity to "hear" input to the other floors and to maintain an attitude of listening decreases according to the ease that we are able to mobilize energy in those other floors. If, for example, a listener has Harmonizer on his sixth floor and an individual addresses him from his Harmonizer Base, the listener will probably have problems "hearing" and responding to the emotional content of the message.

Some people experience a "Phase change". Research shows that 70% of the population phase at least once. Phasing is when we experience life from another floor. A Phase is a movement to and experiencing of the next "floor" of a person's personality condominium. Phasing may explain why some of us experience feeling differently about life, as if we have somehow changed.

Motivation is driven from the Phase. It is the psychological need of Phase which triggers our daily decisions.

Often we experience or live through a Phase change when, for an extended period or time, we show the characteristics of a Personality Type different from that of the Base.

Phase change is possible five times in a lifetime (1% of the population).

Intense and long-term stress can provoke Phase change.

3. Learn How to "Process Communicate"

3.1 Can One Really Change and Evolve in a Lifetime?

We are OK as we are, and of course, fortunately, we can change if we decide to change. We can positively change numerous things, such as our daily communications practices, how we meet our needs, how we look at others, and even attenuate the unconscious impact of our negative scripts.

This is what those that go through a PCM coaching procedure or one of the numerous seminars offered worldwide help us to achieve.

3.2 How Long Does It Take to Change?

It depends on three things, excluding, of course, the quality of the coach or trainer:

1. The level of self-awareness of the person wishing to change and the stage of his or her personal development. (We shall later speak of the four domains of personal development);

2. The **level of personal involvement and investment**, and finally,

3. The **nature of the changes** desired.

A three or four-day seminar will be enough to add new communication skills, such as how to put our case effectively and select words to make oneself heard by people, who up to that point had seemed unreceptive.

One hour spent reading this very book might be enough to provide a different, more acute, and tolerant frame from which we view others.

Working alone or with a coach for several sessions after a seminar will help us to develop better stress-management strategies for someone who previously found it difficult to contain his or her distress. ("I can't help it; in these situations, I get mad.")

We could say that a whole lifetime seems a reasonable amount of time to develop PCM skills. However, don't confuse the potential to change some specific aspect of our behavior in our daily lives that may require a few hours or a few weeks to achieve depending upon the importance and duration of the behavior to be changed, with embracing PCM as a discipline.

> ### "Change the Natural"
>
> We will change only if we are ready. PCM is a discipline that leaves no one person indifferent because it is so pertinent, complete, and predictive. But change requires energy, and it is often that those around us accompany and sometimes help us in the process. Change is not often a natural process; it is not rare to see participants in our seminars leave knowing what is left to do, but not ready or willing do it. One of the first obstacles we may set-up is a recurrent negative belief, "I can't change because our ancient behavior will quickly resurface; so if the natural pattern has such a powerful capacity to create resistance in us, it is the natural that we need to change, step-by-step. It is "enough" to let one's self do it. Moving on the learning curve by practice from Unconscious Incompetence to Conscious Incompetence and then on to Conscious Competence, to Unconscious Competence, thereby creating a new natural way.

4. Who is PCM for?

It's a long list!

Made available to the general public in the United States in the early 1980's and then in Europe by Gérard Collignon through Kahler Communication France, the Process Communication Model offers the "tools" for communication with individuals and groups, as well as for our personal management of distress "trigger mechanisms." Starting from the first observable behavioral signals, Taibi Kahler has determined individual strategies to use in order to avoid miscommunication and to regain the intellectual and emotional availability that are compromised by negative stress.

PCM is for anyone seeking to neutralize the impact of stress on daily behavior. It provides the means to develop our individual resources.

With PCM, **companies** have found a functional and simple approach to energize the management of teams or projects.

We receive frequent requests for guidance and coaching in **management**, the **professions**, and more and more, from **individuals** wishing to take stock of professional or personal projects.

Since 1988, in many European countries, in Japan, and more recently in Africa, Asia and South America, a constantly growing number of **coaches, trainers, recruiting consultants, and psychotherapists** have sought PCM certification in order to make use of profiles or, simply, to form teams. Managers or sales-management teams are also using this model whose applications extend to all fields of human endeavor. Let's say that if human beings are involved, PCM has its place.

In the United States, PCM entered the **American Administration**, which is still tight-lipped on the subject, and **universities** have employed it as tool and even have included it in their curricular development and instruction.

For over thirty years, Joe and Judy Pauley have used an application of PCM with **families**, and, in particular to assist youths with problems in school. Dr. Michael Gilbert now stewards the use of PCM in education in the United States.

A model specifically developed by Rob Wert for legal applications is offered to **lawyers** and professionals in a legal environment.

5. Applications of the Model

5.1 Where am I?

How long will it take me to develop the new skills? To answer this question, it is necessary to establish what degree of time and energy you are ready to commit to yourself. You will find it helpful to look at the table below. It presents the four fields of competencies that PCM provides the means for you to develop in a profound way.

Ask yourself "In which quadrant would I like to develop myself?"

	Self	Others
Knowledge	AWARENESS of Self & one's behavior	AWARENESS of Others & their behavior
Action	Management of Self & one's stress mechanisms	Relationship Management & Team Management

Source: Daniel Goleman and Richard Boyatsis

The field of self-awareness is the absolute point of departure of any move toward personal development. Self-development must begin by knowing one's self. Talk about a truism!

To be more concrete it is a question of three things: being aware of one's emotions and their triggers, having an accurate and undistorted self-image, and having self-confidence. PCM enables precise exploration and rediscovery of one's self with a simple, and above all, verifiable matrix: the Personal Pattern Inventory developed by Taibi Kahler, with and for NASA.

Developing self-management competencies means to act authentically and appropriately in response to one's emotions, relying upon our emotions as important assets in our communication and relationships with others. In PCM the area of psychological needs and the discovery of the predictable stress patterns observable in each of us allow for development in this area.

Awareness of others involves the capacity for empathy and understanding, along with the ability to *decode* their behavioral signals in order to better communicate with them. In this way we can contribute toward the creation of quality relationships. PCM provides subtle and simple-to-use tools for observing signals such as the Personality Parts activated by others, the five behavioral clues, the Communication Channels, and the perceptions indicated by their vocabulary and the preferential themes they address, etc.

Management of relationships is a set of skills that we develop after having acquired the preceding. Included in these outcomes are dramatically improved communication with others; the capacity to act effectively in groups; the development of influencing skills based upon mutual respect; the human aspects of project management; and participation in team building.

Companies use these aspects of PCM, employing not only the aforementioned components and tools, but also the process itself. The name given to this process by Taibi Kahler and NASA during his involvement in astronaut crew selection was Process Communication Management®.

5.2 Personality Pattern Inventory

Originating from a highly researched and validated questionnaire, the Personality Pattern Inventory is the first tool in any training or coaching. The PPI makes a detailed analysis of several important factors of personality and then produces a detailed personal report. These reports are confidential unless clearly stated before the candidate fills the questionnaire. In face-to-face contact with an experienced and certified PCM trainer or coach, together, we make an analysis of this inventory verifying it by using the six components through observation and discussion. Only after this do we accept the validity of a profile.

This is the greatest strength of Taibi Kahler's model: the data produced by the profile are all verifiable by the person answering the questionnaire.

If self-awareness is, in fact, the starting point of development, the Personality Pattern Inventory is the essential tool for this, providing a mirror image of how you saw ourselves through our responses to the questionnaire.

On a personal level it facilitates recognition and awareness of strengths, potential, and the means by which one can meet one's own psychological needs. It provides precise indicators of a person's stress level along with the probable causes of the distress.

In the professional world, a PCM Profile occupies more-and-more an important place as a tool in recruitment. It enables prediction of the most favorable environment for performance and fluidity of communication, and conversely which environment will be a source of stress and demonization. It also makes it possible to form efficient teams in which each member has learned how to integrate with the others without losing sight of his or her own specific assets.

5.3 How Does One Take a Personality Pattern Inventory?

The inventory is taken via a questionnaire originally developed and validated with support from NASA. A revalidation of the inventory was completed by United States researchers in 2012. It is available in several languages. The resulting PPI report is among the most well researched and validated profiling tool available today.

With a PCM certified trainer, coach or therapist. See Appendix for contact details.

> ### BEWARE OF IMITATIONS
>
> Did you know that only trainers, coaches or therapists certified by Taibi Kahler or KCI are entitled to disseminate and teach PCM? There are some non-certified and unscrupulous trainers that claim to follow PCM methods; however, they only provide jury-rigged computer generated personality inventories with no scientific validity. Coaches and therapists must be certified through one of the organizations specified. All certified professionals are listed on one of our web sites.
> Credentials of those claiming to be able to use PCM can be verified at www.processcommunication.com.

5.4 Just What Is the Personality Pattern Inventory?

It takes different forms:

The first document, in the form of a graph, is a synthesis and is used as a quick reference in seminars or coaching. It is a visual résumé of the essential information collected by the questionnaire. It is presented in the form of a bar chart showing in one part the order of preference and the amount of available energy for the six Personality Types of an individual. Below this are distress sequences, i.e. the probable pattern of behavior under stress of this same person.

The PCM Profile is a fifty-page document describing in depth the profile of the person that answered the questionnaire. This is the document that those who filled-in the questionnaire on line receive. It is provided as a matter of course during seminars or private coaching.

There is a third document to identify the profile of a team. It is used in seminars for team building.

Since 2015 additional documents have been offered by Kahler Communications, Inc. for companies and for psychotherapists.

> **PCM Profile**
>
> Profiles for individuals or teams: Includes personality structure;
> Quantified level of available energy on each floor of the building;
> Current Phase and its specific motivators;
> Management styles and preferential Communication Channels;
> Appropriate Perception to use;
> Capacity of the person to communicate with each of the six Personality Types;
> Predictable behavior under light and severe stress.

6. How Can I Learn PCM?

Over five thousand European companies have successfully implemented the Process Communication Model in their training programs and team-building. If you are lucky enough to be in their employment, you may be able to take advantage of it yourself.

More than 2500 hundred consultants, coaches and trainers have been certified all over the world, where most traditional training organizations offer PCM modules.

More and more, employees are profiting from personal coaching, mentoring, and the discovery of PCM.

6.1 How Can a Private Party Train with the Process Communication Model?

Four days of training, generally two two-day sessions, are held two or three weeks apart. Open workshops are offered to private individuals. These sessions are often offered to private individuals at a preferential rate.

A few seminars for families or couples are offered during the year. These seminars concentrate on daily life and family dynamics rather than professional life.

If you look around a little, you will certainly find seminars devoted to the education of children and the counseling of young people with problems in school.

7. PCM in the Company

7.1 How Can Companies Make the Process Communication Model a Part of Their Activities?

The training of executive and middle management staff in the use of communication tools is one of the most frequent uses of PCM in companies. One to 10-day seminars are offered each year by more than 1600 active certified trainers worldwide. Most frequently, the length of sessions is two days working on the foundation followed by another two-day session of training in practical applications anchored with exercises and simulations. The focal point of these seminars is PCM and its application and relevance in the work of team and project managers. It has also been used to help executive teams unravel communication difficulties in their team.

Continuing education over time is another approach frequently used in large as well as in small & medium-sized companies. The principle is to offer an initial team-building seminar, followed by modules on specific problems such as conflict management, mediation, speaking in public, stress management, project management, etc. – themes that respond to the needs identified for certain groups of colleagues. With the aid of PCM, over time these groups develop their collective and personal career paths, the common thread being their PCM training. Companies are thus able to create a common language and a shared communication ethic while retaining a personal dynamic, and in so doing, developing not only the effectiveness of teams, but also developing individuals.

Coaching using PCM has, since the beginning of the millennium, experienced ever-growing expansion because of, on the one hand, the trend of companies willing to channel resources toward developing their managerial staffs and, on the other, the development of PCM Coaching as an effective personal development tool.

7.2 What Takes Place in Process Communication Model Seminars or Training Sessions?

Typically PCM seminars are densely packed; they invite reflection and assessment which also often leads to self-discovery, as well as practice through exercises.

The most popular programs are the three/four day, delivered in two modules consisting of a two-day workshop, followed by a second module of one or two days depending on the objectives of the seminar. A three-consecutive-day workshop is also frequently used, delivering the material and exercises in a slightly denser format.

In the modular approach, the first two days are devoted to the discovery of the intra and interpersonal communication process (between self and self, then between self and others) and then the six Personality Types.

To finish, the PCM tool box is opened to work on two essential dimensions:

- The **Psychological Needs of individuals**, keys to motivation, stress and distress;
- **Channels and Perceptions,** keys to language, working out misunderstandings, and tools of essential contacts.

Generally during the first day, participants receive the results of their individualized Personality Pattern Inventory, which serves as the indispensable pedagogical tool for the seminar.

Program of a typical two-day seminar

The Six Personality Types
    Base Personality
    Current Phase of the individual, means of motivation

Distribution of the Individualized Inventory

Channels of Communication
    Discovery of the five Communication Channels
    Use of the different Channels
    Exercises

The Six Perceptions
    Discovering the six Perceptions
    Use of the right language with others
    Exercises

Psychological Needs
    Recognizing the eight Psychological Needs
    Learning to meet them positively
    Knowing how to identify their symptoms
    Testing and experimenting with each of these needs

The *Elevator*
    Developing ease of relationship management
    Using the resources of each floor
    Increasing one's capacities for healthy adaptation
    Exercises

The follow-up days are devoted to stress mechanisms and management.

The longer the time given to the practice, the more stress management tools the participants take with them and the more they learn how to deal with the conscious and unconscious mechanisms of manipulation.

Minimum Program
Part two of a seminar

***Drivers* (Behavior Under Light Stress)**
    Introduction to the five Drivers
    Knowing how to identify them
    Learning how to manage them so as to avoid Second-Degree stress problems of miscommunication.
    Exercises

Failure Mechanisms (Distress Behavior, 2nd Degree Stress)
    Learning the six Failure Mechanisms
    Identifying their consequences on professional and personal life
    Setting out an intervention strategy to avoid them

Testimonial: "Process Communication Model enables a management team to focus on the same project."

Astronaut and Cosmonaut Marcos Pontes has «been there - done that». He knows that it takes exceptional social-emotional intelligence to lead teams in High Risk, High Stress Environments. That is why he became a certified trainer in the Process Communication Model. Hear what he has to say about PCM:

«The Process Communication Model is a powerful tool for various activities. Throughout all my career as a pilot and astronaut, my life has always been literally in the hands of my team. Having a tool like PCM allows a great communication efficiency, which is one of critical points for team working». - Marcos Pontes - Soyuz TMA 8 - ISS Expedition 13- 2006.

On several occasions in your career you have made use of PrCM, will you tell us about the highlights of your experience as CEO of Bouygues Télécom?

I met Gérard Collignon at the time of the creation of Bouygues Télécom at the end of 1994, when the board of Bouygues Télécom was being formed. I decided to include a Process Communication module in our first seminar because I felt that taking the time to discover and understand ourselves would be an asset in the future workings of the Board. My hopes were immediately rewarded because this method for the mastery of interpersonal communication does not judge the psychological characteristics of individuals, but rather it recognizes them as rich and diverse assets for the group. The reaction was so favorable that the Process Communication vocabulary has become a part of our daily life, and that our partners, seeing the positive atmosphere created by the Board requested that they too be initiated. Mastery of good interpersonal communication has become an integral part of the management culture of Bouygues Télécom. This was fortuitous, because it coincided with the company's values!

What have been the effects engendered by this method and the problems, met during and after the training sessions? How did you solve them?
Positive effects, because awareness has a double effect: better understanding of one's self, and immediately better communication with one's environment. During the training phase, I always saw groups wondering if these "techniques" wouldn't be a little "manipulative." That led to discussions from which it emerged, in general, that responding to the needs of the other party is an additional asset for convincing and inviting better collaboration and therefore, leads to us being more effective. Being aware of the mechanics of a blockage of an exchange, and knowing how to choose a form that will satisfy the other party is, in the end, fairly easy. However, this must be encouraged because our old habits can easily take over again. The manager must stay the course, but it is a requirement that one not lose sight of the needs of the general public, because the clients bring you to order, demonstrating their satisfaction and in some case going as far as to thank you: happiness!

7.3 How to Become a Process Communication Model Certified Trainer and Be Able to Use the Personal Pattern Inventory?

Those seeking certification must go through Kahler Communication Inc. Prior experience in training is preferable but not obligatory.

The modules are as follows:
Module 1: Core Topics
Module 2: Advanced seminar
Module 3: Five to eight days of certification, an oral examination with one Master Trainer

8. VOCATIONAL APPLICATIONS OF THE PROCESS COMMUNICATION MODEL

Apart from trading and certifying certified trainers, KCI has set up three other areas of certification: coaching, psychotherapy with the Process Therapy version, and HR/recruitment and career guidance specialists.

8.1 Process Communication Model Coaching®

This qualifying training for individual and team coaching is intended for those professional coaches or those in the process of being trained who wish to incorporate PCM into their individual coaching methodology.

PCM used in the context of coaching is a powerful model for those being coached to achieve self-development:
- Self-knowledge and self-awareness;
- The understanding of one's behavior under stress and the acquisition of the tools to prevent or manage it;
- The capacity to analyze communication strategies in order to more readily reach professional and personal objectives;

- Relational confidence and charisma

Self-knowledge is facilitated by the study of one's Personal Pattern Inventory®. The coach will use his/her knowledge of PCM to:
Adapt the intervention strategy to those being coached;
Make an analysis, using the model, of the difficulties they encounter and then to develop plans of action aimed at helping them to resolve these difficulties.

This training thus enables someone having previously been coached in the use of PCM questionnaires to individualize their interventions as a foundation to be even more effective coaches and to apply PCM in their work of questioning and post-coaching follow up.

A three-day qualifying module for specialization in team coaching is also offered by Kahler Communications, Inc.

8.2 Process Therapy Model

This certification-training period of two sessions of three consecutive days is for psychotherapists, psychiatrists, clinical psychologists, general practitioners and specialists, social workers (educators, social assistants ...), and benevolent aides (palliative care, guidance ...). It offers a profile (TASP) developed by Taibi Kahler.

There are some prerequisites:
- Proving a list of initial professional education/training (diploma(s), certificate(s)...) and continuing education (attestations); (to qualify to use the profile tool you must be a licensed practitioner);
- A minimum of three years in the field of personal assistance;
- A person's having undergone personal therapy or personal development.

Those wishing to register for this course are first given a private interview to validate the prerequisites and evaluate their motivation.

Objectives for professionals in personal assistance:
- Use the Process Therapy Model in personal assistance;
- Know how to interpret the Personal Pattern Inventory follow up (TASP);
- Gather information of content and procedure in an assistance interview;
- Establish a treatment plan using the Process Therapy Model;
- Conduct interviews and the assistance procedures in the light of the personality structure;
- Use appropriate therapeutic tools taking into account the personality of the client

8.3 Process Communication Model Recruitment

These two training sessions, three consecutive days, for qualification are for heads of HR, heads of recruiting, recruiting consultants or heads of Employment/Mobility.

The prerequisites for this certification are:
- At least three years of practice in recruitment or career guidance activities, in a consulting office or inside a company;
- Conduct recruitment with at least one tool other than interviewing;
- Adherence to a charter of ethics and professional practices

Those wishing to register for this course are first given a private interview to validate the prerequisites and evaluate their motivation.

The objectives for a professional recruiter:
- Apply the PCM in the framework of his/her recruiting practice;
- Establish the candidate profile using PCM and working from the job description/person specification with those concerned in the recruiting mission;
- Know how to conduct a PCM recruitment interview;

- Gather useful and usable information for the evaluation of candidacies using PCM;
- Analyze the information and observations stemming from the results of the Personality Pattern Inventory interview;
- Know how to formulate the diagnosis of the evaluation of the concerned candidacy;
- Learn how to write up PCM evaluation report;
- Acquire the techniques for presentation of the evaluation to candidates and to the deciders concerned with the recruitment.

Additional information is available online at www.kahlercommunications.com.

Chapter 3

The Process Communication Model and the Six Personality Types

1. An Overview of the process Communication model

1.1 The Personality Base

Every individual has one of the six types of personalities predominating in their personality structure: *Persister*, the type linked to values and opinions, *Thinker*, the type linked to analytical thinking and organization, *Harmonizer*, the type linked to relationships and feelings, *Rebel*, the type linked to spontaneity and fun, *Imaginer*, the type linked to stepping back to reflect and imagine, *Promoter*, the type linked to stimulation, challenge and action.

The *Base Personality Type* is the predominant personality. It can often be observed soon after birth or before a few months of age; once established, it doesn't change.

The Base Personality Type determines the individual's strengths, key needs, channel of communication and preferred perceptual filtering as well as favorite management style and predictable miscommunication patterns under heavy stress.

1.2 Secondary Personality Characteristics

In addition to everyone's Base type, there are secondary characteristics that come from other Personality Types. Even though these characteristics are not as developed as the Base, they are available and can be used as additional resources when needed.

The more we use these characteristics, the more we expand the flexibility of our communication style and enhance our potential.

Individuals that develop and evolve positively are those that know how to use these five other characteristics appropriately when needed.

1.3 Phase and Phase Change

In addition to our Base personality, we have a *personality Phase type* that can change over a lifetime. *(For some 30% of people, the Base and Phase are the same and does not change in their lifetimes. This is neither good nor bad; it is simply a statistically observed phenomenon.)*

The Psychological Needs of the Phase can be explained by this play on words: We say that to be in *Phase* with one's self, others and life, the Psychological Needs of the personality *Phase* must be met. From observation we will see that when Phase needs are not met, we enter into stress and display unproductive and negative behavior.

Some people (70% of the population) experience one or more major changes of their sources of *psychological motivation* in their lifetimes. When such a "change" is experienced, a Personality Type different from the Base becomes the determining force of the principle motivation for the individual concerned. We call this the *Phase type* or (*Phasing*).

When moving to a new Phase, the person experiences both the new Psychological Needs and the stress patterns of this new phase.

A Phase lasts at least two years, sometimes a lifetime. Intense and long-lasting stress may provoke a Phase change.

> ### The Personality Condominium
>
> In PCM we represent an individual's personality structure as a six-floor building (In the USA this is called a condominium).
> This image enables us to put the Base personality on the ground floor and say that the other Personality Types are layered above it with the furthest away on the top floor.
> In a training session, the participants speak of their structures in these terms saying, for example, "I am a Rebel type on the fourth floor."

Figure 1 – Personality Building

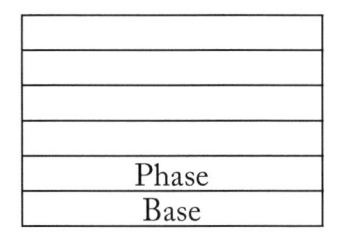

Phase
Base

For this diagram we have placed the individual's current phase on the second floor. Statistical studies show that 70% of the population has phased at least once (as in the diagram above) and 35% more than once. We call these former Phases a stage and the current one the Phase.

1.4 The Elevator Principle, or "Six Characters in Search of Energy"

> I have Phased twice and therefore, my motivation is invested in the needs of my present Phase.

When I am doing well, I can visit all the floors of my condominium; when under stress I act as if I am stuck in my lower Base and Phase floors unable to leave. I lack the energy to mobilize my resources.

When the needs of our Base and Phase floors are met, we easily take the elevator up to the floors that correspond to our secondary characteristics.

If these needs are not met or are frustrated, the elevator is "out of order."

We will experience problems "going upstairs." Sometimes we may tend to display the negative behaviors of our Base and/or Phase Personality types in order to meet these needs.

Figure 2 – Elevator Principle

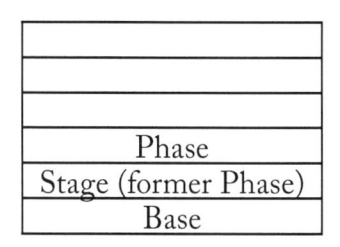

Phase
Stage (former Phase)
Base

The elevator is out of order when I am under stress, that is to say when my Phase and Base needs are not met or are frustrated, when I foster negative thoughts, or simply when I am tired. At such times I seem to lack the drive to shift my energy into other parts of my personality.

2. Personality types

According to Taibi Kahler's model, a Personality Type is defined by a body of information, coherent with itself, that connects a single existential question to a series of observable behaviors, probable skills and a predictable stress pattern.

Each Personality Type corresponds to, among others:
Behavior patterns, attitudes, preferential modes of action,

environmental styles, etc.

Favored perceptual frame of reference as to how we see the world;

Preferred Channels of Communication that enable individuals to connect and to avoid "traps" leading to conflict or passiveness;

Interaction styles, the way we like to interact with groups and express our leadership;

Psychological Needs; meeting these Psychological Needs enables the mobilization of energy and serves to motivate the individual. When not met they characterize our own very personal ways of entering into stress and how we go about seeking a way out of it;

Predictable behavior patterns linked to three progressively greater degrees of intensity of distress.

> A frequent warning for people new to PCM is to avoid considering Personality Type as a definitive description of a person. PCM ethics favors benevolence and the avoidance of labelling others. Labelling people would have the opposite effect.

In the following pages, we present, as if they were real people, Personality Types with their qualities, preferred communication modes, and their predictable behaviors under stress. These are offered as "sketches" rather than photographs.

A file gives the essential information; then a portrait taken from real life helps us to better perceive what this means in daily life. These portraits are "caricatures" in the best sense of the word; everything is exaggerated to see better, but everything is nonetheless an impression of what a person having only one floor in his building would be like.

In passing, I thank my colleague and friend Pierre Agnese, master trainer at Kahler Communication France, for the amusing portraits that he kindly wrote for me to include in this work.

Of course, any resemblance to people that you know, though coincidental, would not be less amusing!

Remember, even at the risk of repeating myself, but this is very important, these portraits are of "pure" types, and each of us is a mixture of all these characteristics in "real life."

2.1 Harmonizer Type

Compassionate, warm and sensitive.
Close, genuine, and attentive relationships are the *sine qua non* of his/her motivation.
Sees the world through the filter of **emotions and feelings.**
An **intuitive** Personality Type that generally displays difficulty in rationally explaining the origins of his/her intuition ("I can't find the right words ... I don't know how to explain ... that's how I feel! it"). In general, a listener, that has the satisfaction and well-being of the other person at heart.
Needs and offers a **benevolent management** style and takes pains to create a warm, close, and friendly team atmosphere.
Prefers communication based on **personal attention.**
Is uncomfortable in **"emotionally cool" environments** and better off in harmonious environments that offer satisfaction to the senses.

2.1.1 To Help with Motivation

Show understanding of what he/she feels and encourage with warmth. Offer true moments of friendly closeness.

2.1.2 Under stress

1st degree: Tends to overadapt and over care. Lack of assurance and firmness in decision-making. Can no longer manage to say "No."

2nd degree: Feels victimized, says "Yes" to everything without being able to do it and in the end will make inadvertent and "stupid" errors leading to lack of credibility.

2.1.3 *Communicating Effectively with a Harmonizer Type*

Be genuinely interested in him/her.
Display understanding, attentive listening and compassion in difficult moments.
Together warmly seek for solutions that enable progress.
Assure him/her of one's support and availability.

Portrait of Joe, Harmonizer

Joe is a young man, very attentive to others, a listener, and understanding.

His welcoming smile strikes one immediately. When he speaks to me, his eyebrows seem to go up to make an even warmer smile.

Even on the phone when I call him I hear a sigh of satisfaction: "Hey, Pete, how are you?"

He says, "How are you?" as if he had just opened a book to his favorite chapter.

When you arrive at Joe's, he always makes sure that you feel at home and covers you with attention. And if he knows that you like chocolate, you can expect quite soon to be offered some.

Joe first perceives people and things through his emotions. He feels first. He explores with his heart and would not argue with the author of the Little Prince, Antoine de Saint-Exupéry when he says, "One only sees well with the heart."

Joe needs to feel unconditionally accepted for whom he is.

He is also fond of food and is a gourmet that loves to cook not only for his own pleasure, but also the pleasure of his friends as well. Love handles betray his love of the arts of the table. But be careful not call attention to these pronounced curves.

When subjected to light pressure, Joe tends to say "Yes" to please his colleague. He will, for example, make a detour to pick up a friend even if it is inconvenient. Saying "No" becomes a problem for him.

Under heavier pressure he will tend overadapt because he feels guilty or he is afraid of no longer being liked. His thinking is no longer very clear. Trying to arrange situations, he does things that go beyond the wishes of others, and despite his good intentions sometimes makes errors.

He is sometimes, according to him, unjustly "sent packing."

Joe presents the characteristics of the Harmonizer type as does 30% of the population 75% being women.

His existential questions are: "Am I loveable? Am I worthy of being liked? Am I doing all I can to ensure that others like me?"

A female collaborator used to say to me: "But, I can't say "no" to clients when they ask me for a sponsorship; they won't like me any more if I do will they?"

2.2 The Thinker Type

Is logical, responsible and organized.
Reaching objectives is the number one motivation.
Looks for **facts**, measurable and verifiable information.
Thinks and analyzes before **acting**.
Needs a **democratic management** style and to be consulted and informed. Also uses the democratic style.
Prefers communication based on exchange of information.
Dislikes the unexpected and improvisation.

2.1.1 To Help with Motivation

Provide him/her with all the information needed, ask for his/her analysis of the situation.
Structure and plan with him/her the steps to be taken to reach the objective.

2.1.2 Under Stress

1st degree: Attempts to be perfect; provides too many details and too much information.

2nd degree: Over-controls, will tend to verify everything several times. No longer trusts and imposes his/her methods. Can become frustrated, angry and attacking.

2.1.3   *Communicating Effectively with a Thinker Type*

Get directly and seriously to the point.
Give all the necessary information and testing (avoid making generalizations).
Be on time and see that time is used wisely.
Emphasize what is working well; together develop precise plans based on reliable data; set clear realistic objectives that, if possible, are proposed by him/her.

Portrait of Sam, Thinker

Sam is a friend of mine. His strengths are his capacity for analysis and his ability to structure facts and ideas and find a rationale.
Even the personal organization, his time and his projects are models of structure.
Anecdotally, he explains during a dinner his career plan, the time devoted to each stage, how much time before his first real estate purchase, when and how these things were going to unfold according to his plan.
The only thing he couldn't program was when his first child would be born; but, he told me, "We're working on it!"!
I remember one day he told me, when we were barely 20 years old, that he had calculated the amount of his retirement if things went according to plan (he had even taken care to use a reasonably predictable curve of his career progression).
In all situations, Sam starts by thinking, by looking for the facts and information in order to classify them and draw conclusions from them.
Sam also needs temporal reference points, time and time structure is important to him.

Sam is a CPA and has just been taken on by a company that has given him new responsibilities. For him, it represents a promotion. He breezed through all the recruitment steps and was chosen for his competence and the quality of his observation and thinking.

Sam is very satisfied with this because it responds to one of his fundamental motivations: being recognized for his work.

Balance sheet time is when the pressure mounts in Sam's job. Under this pressure he begins to have doubts about the professionalism of his collaborators. He tends to take all the files over himself to be sure the job is done well.

And if the pressure increases, he takes the time to verify everything and no longer delegates anything, stays in the office until 10 p.m. and returns at 7 a.m. the next day. To finish up he comes in on Saturday and doesn't go home until he has finished, and verified everything several times. I have seen him do this.

One day, seeing him very tense, I suggested offhandedly that he relax and not take things so much to heart. I saw his face darken and he explained, at times severely, that life is not made to have fun and that the work had to be done and that it didn't get done on its own and that he is the only one who can do it correctly ... etc.

Sam presents the characteristics of the Thinker Type as does 25% of the population 75% of which are men.

His existential questions are: "Am I competent? Have I acquired the knowledge and the know-how to survive?"

2.3 The Persister Type

Is conscientious, dedicated, and observant.
Likes to take on a **mission** and see it through to the end.
Is a woman or a man of **convictions**
Is tenacious and wants to finish what he/she starts.
Sees the world through the filter of his/her **opinions.**
Asking for his/her opinion is of great importance to him/her.
Acts effectively especially when he/she **believes** in the decision taken.
Needs a **democratic management** style and manages using this style.
Prefers communication based on **exchange of opinions.**
Needs to feel **respected.**

2.3.1 *To Help with Motivation*

Listen to him/her.
Respect his/her point of view; emphasize the positive aspects of it.

2.3.2 *Under Stress*

1st degree: Becomes negative. Sees more of what is wrong than what is right. Expects others to be perfect. Is less able to make positive observations.
2nd degree: Goes on crusades (tries to impose his/her point of view, no longer listens, interrupts). Develops a rather "paranoid" side ("Those that aren't with me are against me").

2.3.3 *Communicating Effectively with a Persister Type*

Listen to him/her.
Ask for his/her opinions.
Seek his/her advice and counsel, and listen to the end.
Avoid giving unsolicited advice; check if he/she believes it is needed.
Emphasize the points of agreement rather than the points of disagreement.
Practice rephrasing his/her point of view. To endorse a point of view, he/she must feel understood.

Sylvia is an Orthopedic Surgeon and also a Persister

She is a conscientious and committed woman.
When she speaks with you, she looks at you intently, with furrows between her eyes that seem to accentuate her words. In French plastic surgery, these are called "lion's wrinkles."
When she comes to dinner without fail, she will affirm her convictions as to the benefits of surgery, especially her specialty.

Her assets are her strength of conviction and her ability to defend values.

This strengthens her determination and enables her to move mountains.

Sylvia sees the world through the filter of her convictions.

She needs be recognized for the quality of her commitment and for the opinions she holds dear.

If Sylvia is submitted to light pressure, she will tend to point out what is going badly much more than what is going well.

For example, she points out that, according to her, the current government does not further the exercise of her profession. When she comes to my home after a bad day, she will take pleasure in commenting: "Hey, I see you still haven't changed your tires …"

If she enters a discussion topic where the pressure is the strongest, she no longer listens; she interrupts, and tries to impose her ideas as if her reputation depended upon them. I am less reassured when I see her like this.

She expresses vehement criticisms of the lack of comprehension of the needs of her profession. She asserts, "You'll see, tomorrow, there won't be any surgeons for your children and grandchildren."

As for me, I had better change my tires if I want to avoid being labelled irresponsible!

Sylvia presents the characteristics of the Persister Type, as does 10% of the population 75% of which are men.

Her existential questions are, "Am I worthy of confidence? Would people be ready to trust me to guide them?"

2.4 The Imaginer Type

Is calm, reflective, and imaginative.

Appreciates the quiet of solitary moments to imagine the world and explore in his/her head the world of possibilities.

Needs clear, brief and precise **instructions** and likes to have his/her own space (even small) in which to reflect in order to work effectively

Has a great deal of imagination and needs outside motivation to get into action (without instructions can remain inactive).

Needs an **autocratic** management style.

2.4.1 To Help with Motivation

Tell him/her clearly what is to be done.
Use his/her capacities of imagination and liking for in-depth analysis of situations. Needs time to be alone (solitude)

2.4.2 Under Stress

1st degree: Becomes passive, withdrawn, and reclusive. Gets involved in projects and doesn't finish them.
2nd degree: Waits passively. Becomes invisible, physically disappears.

2.4.3 Communicating Effectively with a Imaginer Type

Respect his/her quiet and effective rhythm (effective because of the quiet).
Have brief and directive exchanges.
Indicate precisely what is expected of him/her.
Show that you understand, his/her need for solitude.

Portrait of Ronnie an Imaginer

When my in-laws speak of Uncle Ronnie, the calm and serenity he exudes are often evoked. It's true that Ronnie is a very calm and introspective man; a calm that radiates positively on all the family.
Having often spoken with him, I know that inside he is anything but calm, but his emotions rarely manifest themselves
He perceives people and situations through the filter of his fertile imagination.
Ronnie likes it when other people propose activities, for example, an invitation to spend a weekend at the house, having him light the barbecue, or just go for a walk …

Everyone in the family knows that Ronnie often needs to be alone. In fact, one of his favorite hobbies is to go off alone to hike in the Pyrenées for a few days. It's his quiet space, especially in the winter when the snow covers everything and mutes the noises. The white calm suits him. There he meditates. He is in his own interior universe. Conditions there are harsh, but Ronnie never complains.

In stressful situations Ronnie's face seems to close, and he will tend to appear to withdraw from the situation. He retreats into himself. Physically he is there but everything indicates that he has left for his interior world.

When the pressure increases Ronnie's retreat is complete: physically and psychologically. He waits passively at home or in the mountains on hikes that get longer and longer.

Another sign that Ronnie is under heavy stress is when runs into difficulties with his tasks and then seems unable to finish them.

Uncle Ronnie presents the characteristics of the Imaginer Type, as does 10% of the population of which 60% are women.

His existential questions are, "Am I wanted? Am I welcome? What do people want from me? Is someone waiting for me somewhere?" Another example is my friend Karine. We always ask her to participate in an activity ahead of time. She often says "No." The other day we forgot to call her before going to the restaurant. She told us that she was disappointed to have been forgotten.

2.5   The Promoter Type

Is adaptable, resilient and charming
Likes challenges, novelty, immediate results
Acts on **impulse** and **adapts** according to the result.
Has a large capacity to adapt (is sometimes compared to a chameleon).
Doesn't like *reporting* and sitting in on long meetings based on exchange of ideas or sharing information.
Is a loner and a go-getter.
Needs an **autocratic management** style. Manages autocratically.
Give him/her a challenge and he/she is off and running.

2.5.1 *To help with motivation*

Accept his/her go-getter side (which sometimes leads directly into a wall)
Be firm with him/her, do not be over-flexible.

2.5.2 *Under Stress*

1st degree: Can't put up with people that he/she sees as "dependent" … "It's not my problem." "I don't want to know." "Here, it's every man for himself …"
2nd degree: Takes risks with his/her physical health and security (drives too fast for example). Manipulates, "His beautiful words are mostly hot air…"

2.5.3 *Communicating Effectively with a Promoter Type*

Recognize his/her "exploits."
Accept his/her "boastful" side.
Be firm and stimulate with challenges.
Accept his/her lack of enthusiasm for rigorous organization and systematic *reporting*.

Portrait of Philip a Promoter

Philip is the managing director of a subsidiary of an international group. He is a very persuasive man brimming with energy

He frequently travels all over the world and confessed to me that he doesn't know what "jet lag" is.

Philip adores state-of-the-art and luxury. He has a life style, which is often above his means. Nothing is too fashionable: when he goes away for the weekend it is often on the spur of the moment and in a private jet, a luxury hotel on Capri, a sports convertible, preferably red…

He was one of first to have a digital video telephone and access to satellite communication. He leaves it on at all times during board meetings, and invariably the Elvis rock and roll ring-tone goes off to his immense pleasure.

He has an astonishing capacity to be firm and direct. When he arrives at the headquarters of this moribund subsidiary, he starts taking decisions, acting first and then adapting in response to the results of his action.

Philippe has a great need for strong stimulation. He finds, for example, weekly board meetings boring. As a result, before beginning one of them he asks everyone to express themselves, and not to hesitate to express reservations, adding, "That'll add a little spice and action!"

When under pressure he tends not to put up with dependent people. On bad days you can only ask him what time it is!

Last year during a seminar when I gave him feedback from his colleague asking him to be more involved and present he exclaimed, "All these people that can't fend for themselves! Do I need anyone?"

When the pressure intensifies, Philip tends to provoke others manipulating them emotionally by excessive challenges even if it means taking risks himself.

Philip presents the characteristics of the Promoter Type as does 5% of the population, 60% of which are men.

His existential questions are, "Am I alive? Am I really living the moment to the fullest?"

2.6 The Rebel Type

Is creative, spontaneous, and playful.

Loves to **play**, even when working.

Life is a playground. Is well schooled in the practice of *carpe diem, (Enjoy the day; or seize the day)*, and let's take life as it comes.

Reacts to what he/she experiences: Likes or doesn't like, wants to do it or doesn't want to do it.

Motivation is, for the most part, linked to the quality of the contact he/she has in relationships with others and all his/her colleagues ("They're cool or a pain in the a.").

Needs a **stimulating** and playful environment where he/she can freely express **creativity**.

Needs a "**laissez faire**" management style and tends to use this style as well.

2.6.1 To Help with Motivation

Be serious without taking one's self too seriously!
One is not overly serious; one finds the "fun" way to reach ones objectives.
Let the fun begin!
If it's impossible, it's possible.
Use your sense of humor.

2.6.2 Under Stress

1st degree: May delegate inappropriately (give tasks to people who are not sufficiently trained for example); Uses the word "Try" as opposed to "I will," or "I will not." Looks tense as if straining to understand.

2nd degree: Blames. Rejects responsibility for the impact of his/her actions and words on others ("It's not my fault!") Blames others, (If it weren't for him/her). Exports his/her anger.

2.6.3 Communicating Effectively with a Rebel Type

Joke and make things less dramatic; this is an excellent means to broach the most delicate of subjects.
Accept his/her distaste for convention. Allow room to be different.
Encourage expression and putting new ideas into action.

Portrait of Polly the Rebel

What Polly's office colleagues appreciate is her spontaneity, her capacity to instantly find the correct phrase, the clever repartee that creates a good mood on the entire floor.

From her sparkling eyes, one can always be sure she has come up with a new original solution for a tender offer. It is true that Polly tends to look for fun anywhere and anytime.

For example, three months ago the office was being refurbished. Well, the three workers that were there could count on her to punctuate the sanding, and painting sessions and other activities with a joke every twenty minutes.

Polly reacts immediately to situations and people. Her perception filter is made above all from her reactions. She adores or she detests, that's it. In fact, Polly lives in the present.

By herself, Polly could not work efficiently for any length of time; to function well she has a strong need for multiple and invigorating contacts with others.

We organized a dinner with friends, and one of them was one of Polly's colleagues. She told me, "In fact, if Polly is alone in her office for half an hour, she will suddenly come to see you, talk to you and tease you. It lasts five minutes and she is happy; she returns to her office whistling. One would say she comes to recharge her batteries with us."

If Polly is required to work in a directive and demanding system, she will tend to sigh, get bored, or complain. For example, at a meeting a Thinker manager that might say, "For the end-of-vacation seminar, meet at 8 o'clock in front of the airport; don't forget your passports and formal dress for Tuesday night's gala …" If this information comes in the middle of a serious meeting where everyone is working hard, Polly will make a face as if she is trying to understand and her reaction might be, "What! What did he say, a gala, what gala? I didn't understand a word!" With this reaction she is inviting others to have contact with her, to explain it to her again.

If her boss continues to push, she will tend to dig in her heels and become unpleasant. A sign that Polly is under pressure is the appearance of an "It's not my fault," followed by a criticism of others who are at fault! "They should have told us sooner for their gala evening and the formal dress; it's just not done blah blah blah…"

Polly presents the characteristics of the Rebel Type as does 20% of the population 60% of which are women.

Her existential questions are: "Am I acceptable? To what extent are you ready to accept my behavior and continue to love me?"

3. How to "Process Communication Model" Listen? Quick Diagnosis

What to listen for in order to recognize the Base and Phase of the other person?

3.1 Identifying the Base

We have a strong tendency to speak and perceive through our Base. It is therefore observation of the Channel and Perception that is most frequently used as they are the key distinguishing criteria: the non-verbal messages such as gestures, facial expressions, posture, speech patterns, tones, and register chosen to express one's self will reveal the Channel and Perception of the Base Type. We also use the words that fit with Channel and Perception.

3.1.1 *Harmonizer Base*

- Preferred Communication Channel: Nurturative.
- Perception: Feelings.
- Warm and comforting tone. Shares. Suggests without imposing. Invites exchange and friendly contact.
- Uses a sensory vocabulary, expresses the experienced and emotions.

3.1.2 *Thinker Base*

- Preferred Communication Channel: Requestive/Informative.
- Perception: thoughts/facts/data.
- Serious. Asks questions or gives information.
- Looks for factual elements. Structure. Method.

3.1.3 *Persister Base*

- Preferred Communication Channel: Requestive/Informative
- Perception: thoughts/opinions.

- Serious. Asks questions or gives information.
- Gives his/her opinion, makes judgements or asks others to take positions.

3.1.4 *Imaginer Base*

- Preferred Communication Channel: Directive likes to be given to him/her: (Opens communication from the channel corresponding to the Personality Type above his/her Base floor:
- Perception: Imaginations (seen as being inactive)
- Is often manually dextrous. Speaks little. Short sentences. Long pauses.

3.1.5 *Promoter Base*

- Preferred Communication Channel: Directive.
- Perception: Actions.
- Strong, firm, determined, frequently uses the imperative.
- Targets the useful, seizes opportunities. Action verbs.

3.1.6 *Rebel Base*

- Preferred Communication Channel: Emotive (playful)
- Perception: Reactions (likes and dislikes).
- Expresses and shows his/her likes and dislikes.
- Energetic, playful or gently provocative.

3.2 Identifying the Phase

We make decisions and we motivate ourselves through our current "Phase."

It is, therefore, the distinguishing Psychological Need: motivation criteria and strongly expressed expectations.

3.2.1 *Thinker Phase*

- Needs structured time and recognition of his/her work accomplishments.
- Quantifies; analyzes; compares; synthesizes.
- Details his/her activities and methods.
- Gives analyses and plans the actions.

3.2.2 *Harmonizer Phase*

- Needs recognition as a person, comfort and sensorial satisfaction.
- Speaks of him/herself openly and is interested in you.
- Demonstrates attentiveness and needs it in return.
- Takes care of his/her sensorial needs by seeking comfort and fleeing from the uncomfortable.

3.2.3 *Persister Phase*

- Needs recognition of the value of his/her opinions and contributions at work.
- Appreciates being asked for his/her opinion. Suggests or gives advice.
- Evokes his/her perseverance at work, ideas and projects, and dedication.

3.2.4 *Imaginer Phase*

- Needs solitude (time and space to think and recharge batteries).
- Speaks little. Moves out of the picture when the occasion arises.
- Listens well, displays peace and calm.

3.2.5   Promoter Phase

- Needs excitement
- Takes risks.
- Displays his/her power and is triumphant about victories
- Challenges him/herself.

3.2.6   Rebel Phase

- Needs positive contacts in a dynamic mode.
- Plays, calls out to others, jokes.
- Makes contact for no special reason. "Just like that …"

The Base and the Phase are determining elements for identifying the keys to the general functioning of an individual, but they do not reveal who that individual is.

In fact, when a PCM profile is drafted after the questionnaire has been completed, the six floors of their building are set out in detail, that is to say how the components of each of the six Personality Types are distributed in the total profile.

The details of the components are presented in the following pages.

The interest of separating the Base and Phase data is obvious when we want to work on the motivation and stress dimensions. It is also very useful in coaching, etc.

CHAPTER 4

The Essential Components of the Personality Structure

When we receive our PCM profile, we discover that we are a mix of all six Personality Types.

Each component is then analyzed and quantified in order to obtain a coherent and sufficiently detailed picture so that we can work on precise aspects rather than a diffuse ensemble.

Each of these aspects is called a component.

Ten components at least are analyzed and quantified in the PCM profile. We will examine six in detail in the following pages:

Interaction Styles;
Personality Parts;
Perceptions;
Communication Channels;
Psychological Needs;
Environment.

Additional elements of the PCM Profile not found as such in this book are:

The eighteen character strengths (three key behavior skills for each type presented);

The predictability of the behavior pattern under stress presented in the form of a graph and explained in the PCM Profile;

Preferred environment (the environment in which an individual prefers to be, more or less);

> ### Why coaching or training?
>
> As PCM is a communication and situation management model for professional and personal life, it is essential for one to move from discovery of the profile to its practical application with a certified PCM trainer or coach.
> Seminars or coaching permit one to:
> Validate his/her profile by testing in real life the information contained in the profile.
> Develop his/her communication to be a competent communicator with all the six types.
> Pinpoint his/her own psychological needs and to develop personal ways to meet them in order to avoid the dysfunctional behavior linked to failure to meet these needs;
> Improve the management of his/her stress;
> Learn how to identify the preferred communication mode of others in order to attune oneself to it;
> Learn how to identify the Psychological Needs of other people to better meet their needs and thereby motivate them;
> Identify how people have miss-communicated and spot the sequence of distress signals of others that lead from misunderstanding to miscommunication and conflict;
> Avoid the manipulative "traps," either conscious or unconscious, offered by others;
> Manage groups or group situations composed of different personality types.

1. Interaction Styles

Each individual tends to use (and to want used with them) a preferred management style according to his/her Base Personality Type.

We identify four management styles:
Autocratic;

Democratic;
Benevolent;
"Laissez-faire."

1.1 Autocratic Style

The autocratic manager is focused on the goal to be reached, a job to be accomplished, and puts people and creativity in the background.

They give orders and directives to colleagues and demands an account of what they do.

Use of this style is effective in urgent situations and where a member of staff needs clear direction. However, for most management situations, it discourages interaction, discussion, and participation.

1.2 Democratic Style

The democratic manager encourages interaction with him/herself as well as within the team.

They request information and encourages reflection and believes that others may have useful ideas and contributions to make. This manager retains authority and makes the decisions. It is a useful style for managing people who are self-motivating, know their jobs well, and want to develop their potential. On the negative side, this style may lack enough direction for people who are inexperienced or who need direction.

1.3 Benevolent Style

This management style describes a manager more oriented toward people than toward the task.

For this manager, emotions and the quality of relationship influence the result. They think that people are efficient when they feel good at work. This manager fosters team spirit. They encourage interaction between people and promote the "feeling" of belonging in the team.

1.4 "Laissez-faire" Style

Even though the manager using a "laissez-faire" style management holds the authority, he/she encourages colleagues to assume as much authority and responsibility as they can handle.

They place themselves at the same level as others and deem that they know what they have to do, then sit back and enjoy the team.

1.5 Individualistic Management

The preferred management style of each of us may give good results with some Personality Types but may not be suitable with others.

This is why flexibility of management styles makes it possible to meet the needs of everyone and generate effectiveness.

The manager that knows how to individualize his/her style encourages communication, develops productivity, reduces dissatisfaction and stress factors, and optimizes the functioning of the company's staff. Recognizing the preferred management style of a member of their team, they are able to avoid the trap of using an inappropriate management style.

Implementing this style requires a great deal of personal investment of energy. The individualistic manager must be aware of the personality types of colleagues and takes responsibility for guiding the communication process. A useful tip is to remember, of the four types of management styles, only 15% of the population (Promoters 5% and Dreamers 10%) respond well to the Autocratic Style.

2. Personality Parts

A Personality Part is a coherent set of verbal and non-verbal behavior that we use when we communicate.

In Transactional Analysis Personality Parts are called Ego States. In seminars, I like to compare Personality Parts to a "state of mind."

At certain times we are in our thinking part, at other times, we want to let our hair down and be carefree, and at other times, we desire to take care of those we love and to give the best of ourselves.

In PCM five positive personality parts are identified (four of which correlate to Personality Types). These parts are recognizable because they are expressed with the following indicators, or behavioral clues:

Words

Tones

Gestures

Postures

Facial Expressions

When we observe at least three of these indicators, we can conclude that the corresponding personality part is activated, and this also means one of the associated personality types is being accessed.

Of these five indicators, the first, words, will be described below when component and perceptions are discussed.

A strong indicator of the quality of our communication is that if we are not communicating from one of these positive personality parts, we are under stress and are not communicating efficiently.

2.1 Director

When we have our energy in the director part, we give orders to the other persons though this part by use of imperatives.

This is not to be confused with negative authority: anger, attack, and threat are absent here.

Prominent in the *Promoter* Type.

Words: "Say..." "Do..." "Tell..." All imperatives, which involve thinking on the other part of the person.

Tones: Firm, non-critical, non-threatening.

Gestures: Almost no gestures.

Postures: Erect.

Facial Expression: Neither raised eyebrows nor a frown. Expressionless.

"Tell me the most important objective in this job" "Bring me the key account files"

2.2 Computer

When we use the computer part, we ask questions and look for data. There are no emotions involved.

From the computer we don't give orders and don't use the imperative but rather formulate clear requests.
Prominent in *Thinker, Persister,* and *Imaginer* Types.

Words: "What...?" "When?" "Will you...?" "Where?" "Is...?" "How...?" and "Who?" Generally every question is asked in a non-emotional and non-critical way.

Tones: Neutral.

Gestures: Almost none.

Postures: Erect, steady.

Facial Expressions: Attentive.

"What time is it?"; "What were your responsibilities in your former job?"; "What do you expect of me?"

2.3 Emoter

When we use the Emoter part, we use the playful and sensitive part of ourselves -- No vengeance, no spite, no teasing, no whims but rather fun and a spontaneous expression of our humorous energy.

You are in your Emoter part when you do fun things and/or you share your positivity with the other person.

The Emoter doesn't make fun "of" others or him/herself in derogatory ways. The Emoter part enables living through difficult situations in a genuine way; it expresses sorrow for the loss of someone close or the end of a relationship, or an expected promotion that didn't go through. Anger, expressed as an authentic personal feeling and not against the other, is also a trait of the Emoter.

Prominent in the *Rebel* Type.
Words: "Great," "Brilliant," "Cool," "I like it" "Love it," "Don't like it"… also lots of slang words.
Tones: Upbeat, energetic, enthusiastic, playful.
Gestures: Animated, lively.
Postures: Relaxed, open, fluid, flexible, dynamic.
Facial Expressions: Smiling, natural, twinkle in the eyes.

"Great tie!" "Brilliant meeting!" "Man am I down!"

2.4 Comforter

When we use the comforter part, we use the warm and sincere part of ourselves; we take care of others; we address the feelings of the other person. We express feelings not thoughts.

Prominent in the *Harmonizer* Type.
Words: "I appreciate you," "You're important to the team and I," "I'm glad that you're with us."
Tones: Soft, gentle, soothing, caring.
Gestures: Hands out, palms up.
Postures: Slightly leaning toward the other person, open.
Facial expressions: Accepting, warm, smiling, gentle open.

"I appreciate you a lot"; "I understand that you're a little stressed, you can share your feelings with me"; "You're a warm person, and I'm glad you're here."

2.5 Protector

When we use the protector part, we aim our interventions at the other person's senses.

The content is not attacking, threatening, or angry. The protector helps us to regain our composure when we may be slightly disturbed or panicky in highly tense emotional situations.

Not characteristic of any particular type. (We may all get panicked at some time in our lives and feel that our emotions are overwhelming us)

Words: All directed at one of the five senses (smell, taste, sight, hearing touch). No threat, attack or anger is present.

Tones: Firm, protective, calm, accepting.

Gestures: Hands and arms outstretched as if resting on the shoulders of a child.

Postures: Calm but firm, sometimes a nod of the head, to affirm it is OK to do as I say.

Facial expressions: Non-critical, a trusting and supportive look

"Look at me; take a deep breath." "Breathe deeply and slowly."

3. Perceptions

Each Personality Type has a unique way of viewing the world. These perceptions are revealed by the words each type uses in discussion, especially the verbs. The language used will give us both new keys to identify the Personality Type along with information as to the best means of communication to use in order to establish a positive rapport and mutual understanding.

Using these perceptions is like pushing on the right lever to open the door of communication.

One of the most frequent sources of misunderstandings comes from the fact that we use a language to communicate that might not be clearly "perceived" by the other.

"Hello, Paul, what do you think of Fellini's new film?"
– Totally brilliant! I had a ball!
– Yes and what did you think about it?"

This kind of "missing" each other occurs daily and is the start of potentially stressful miscommunication. The two people are speaking a different language, much like when an American comes to England where an item of men's clothing that the American refers to as pants, the Englishman calls trousers especially as in England men wear pants as an undergarment. Hence the joke, "In America men wear their pants on the outside." ; We think we are speaking the same language but we may end up misunderstanding each other

3.1   The Perception of "Emotions"

Emotions include feelings, sensations, and our physical and emotional perceptions of our world and relationships. Frequent words are: I love (rather than like), I feel, my intuition says, empathize, I want to share. Those using the perception of emotions love to share the feelings or the "lived experiences" of others.

It is the *favored contact perception of those with the Harmonizer Base* that first experiences the environment through their feelings; it is not unusual that they anticipate what they "feel" others are going to feel especially in difficult situations, and they often consider it essential to begin by stating their feelings'

"I don't feel good about that method." "I would be more comfortable if we tried something different." "I am so glad we found this solution."

3.2   The Perception of "Thoughts"

In PCM we distinguish two areas of "thought."
The perception "thoughts/opinions": it is the *favored contact perception of the Persister Base*. People with a Persister Base need to establish contact with others by giving their opinions; they need the other person to accept their opinions, or at the very least to listen to them and respect them. When they ask a question, one clearly hears from the tone employed what they think. They often begin by seeking to have their opinion validated by the other; hence "leading" questions are often used.

"Don't you think we should try another method?"

The perception "thought, facts, and information" is the *favored perception of the Thinker Base*. People with a Thinker Base prefer to learn and gather all the available information; to analyze and synthesize the facts before drawing a conclusion. So they will question and take the time to analyze before deciding. To understand they analyze.

"What may happen if we tried another method?" "How many sales do we need to break even in the first year?"

3.3   The Perception of "Actions"

In PCM we distinguish three areas of "action."

The perception of "actions/reactions": the *favored perception of the Rebel Base*. People who have a Rebel Base like to establish contact energetically. They express themselves with lots of slang and energy. They want their colleagues to react. "Communicate equals stimulate." If there is no reaction on our part, they will push until we react, going from humor to provocation.

"Hey guys, I guess we could have real fun with this project." "What do you know; we've gotten us a live one!"

The "reflection action" perception is the *favored perception of the Imaginer Base.* People with a strong Imaginer Base need to have a clear set of instructions and parameters for new things to motivate them. If they give the impression that they are lost in their thoughts, they are exploring hypotheses rather than analyzing. They project themselves in the process of doing and "live" in their head what they imagine. They don't necessarily feel the need to implement. This is why in a group these Imaginer Base people don't respond well to direct questions and often appear to simply "not be there." They are caught up with their reflections and imagination, possibly having very inventive ideas, but not communicating them. The Imaginer Base types are always doing something ... in their heads.

The perception "action" is the *favored perception of the Promoter Base*. People with this base type prefer to "shoot from the hip"; to test it before analyzing and who wonder, "What's the bottom line?" "I'll make it work." People with this Base speak in the imperative and quickly become impatient. For them, it is enough to experiment; we'll see. They accept error because it is a part of their system of reference. A mistake is simply an attempt that didn't work. Their vocabulary is direct sometimes crude.

"Just do it and see what happens…"

4. Channels of Communication

Like a CB radio, for two people to communicate, they must be sending and receiving on the same channel.

Using the correct Channel becomes a powerful tool for contact. When we notice that our message (transmission) is not being received, it may be necessary to "re-adjust" our communication by using a different channel.

As with perceptions, PCM indicates four Channels, which enable us to establish or re-establish contact with the other person, plus one emergency Channel. If we use the correct channel, we become more efficient communicators. It is often enough to tune to and transmit on the other person's preferred wavelength.

"Communication takes place when there is an offer and an acceptance in the same Channel." *Acceptance is when the response is "crisp," i.e. clearly matching the opening transmitted signal.*

We have five Channels at our disposal.

4.1 The Directive Channel

Gives clear directions aimed at the "thinking personality part" of the other person.

In order for us to define this channel, the direction must contain no threat or aggression and the objective needs to be achievable.

This Channel correlates to the *Promoter Base Personality Type (who will both respond to this Channel and open in it) and to the Imaginer Base Personality Type (who responds to it)*

"Give me the conclusions of your report next Tuesday."
"Tell me what it will take to get it done by Friday."
"Listen for fifteen minutes, and I'll explain my proposal."

The Imaginer Base type generally opens communication using the Channel of the Personality Type on the flood above their Imaginer Base.

4.2 The Requestive/Informative Channel

Exchanges information. Asks questions. Notice that **"exchanging information"** isn't "imposing information" and isn't a monologue.

This Channel correlates to *Thinker and Persister Personality Base Types.*

"Will you give me the conclusions of your report next Tuesday?"
"How many people do you think it will take to finish this task by Friday lunch time?"
"Do you have fifteen minutes to give me to explain my proposal?"

4.3 The Nurturative Channel

Shows understanding, empathy, and warmth toward the other person.

This Channel is not often employed during a seminar, because it is a question of expressing real concern or tenderness to someone, something that cannot be made up or faked.

This Channel correlates to *Harmonizer personality Base Types*.

"I enjoy working with you, and I'd be happy to hear your report next Tuesday."

"I feel concerned that we may be asking too much of our team, to expect them to finish by Friday."

"I'd love to share my proposal with you; can you spare me fifteen minutes?"

4.4 The Emotive (Playful) Channel

Targets the reactions of the other person. It is an enthusiastic and playful tone with good energy.

It is via this channel that spontaneous energy is exchanged. It is about living in the moment, openly revealing your reactions.

This Channel correlates to *Rebel personality Base Types*.

"Hey let's take a look at you conclusions next Tuesday!"

"Wow! We're going take care of this effectively and in really innovative way. Are you with me?"

"Okey dokey, bet we can tuck up this proposal in fifteen minutes."

4.5 The Interventive Channel

Is used to calm someone who is in a panicked state or who is very distressed.

Uses simple terms aimed at the senses in a firm yet benevolent way.

One thinks here of language used with a terrorized child awakened by a nightmare.

This Channel does not correlate to any specific Personality Type.

"Look at me! Take my hand."
"Take a deep breath and relax."

5. Psychological Needs

Psychological Needs are the cornerstone of our emotional wellbeing.

Our motivation is determined by the Psychological Needs of our present Phase.

Therefore, the Psychological Needs of our Base are the most important. When there has been a period of long-term, non-satisfaction of needs, this becomes our Achilles heel. We are then likely experience a period of severe stress.

We say that motivation is in the Phase and de-motivation is in the Base.

This means that there are two levels to satisfy. The needs of the Base have been important to us throughout our lives and they are the keys to our development. If they are not met, we are in a state of frustration and lose energy and access to our resources. We become "de-motivated."

The needs of our Phase on the other hand, correspond to our present development; when we satisfy our current Phase Needs, we experience high levels of energy. When these needs are met, we are "motivated."

So first nourish the Phase (to be motivated) and then nourish the Base (in order not be de-motivated).

Example from daily life

Mary is in a Harmonizer Phase and Mark, her husband, is in a Rebel Phase.

Their Psychological Needs resemble each other yet are very different. Mary needs recognition as a person and sensory satisfaction to be well, in tune with herself, others and life. Mark needs positive and playful contacts. When they spend Saturday afternoon playing tennis together, their needs are being met. However, once the match is over, Mary prefers to have a cup of hot chocolate in front of the fireplace, while Mark would rather make a surprise visit to one of their friends for a little three-way Nintendo tournament.

In this example, we see that the same activity (a tennis match) can meet different psychological needs: recognition of her as a person because the match is played with her loved one; playful contacts for him because sport is fun, sensorial needs for her because sport is good for the body.

However, after the event Mary (who is in Harmonizer Phase) still needs comfort-after-effort, a sensorial satisfaction; a hot bath and some cozy warm time together by the fire, the latter providing her with recognition as a person (a tender moment together). Whilst Mark nourishes his need for comfort-after-effort with even more contact: a surprise visit to a "buddy" and video games, real fun.

Often, it is how we meet the same, apparently shared, need (here comfort after the effort) that enables us to observe the subtleties of the Psychological Needs of Phase.

Our principal source of motivation is the need of the Phase.

Table 2 – Psychological Needs

NEEDS	PERSONALITY TYPES
Recognition of Person, Sensory Needs	HARMONIZER

Recognition for Work Time Structure	**THINKER**
Recognition of Contribution at Work Recognition of Convictions	**PERSISTER**
Solitude	**IMAGINER**
Excitement	**PROMOTER**
Positive, Playful Contact	**REBEL**

Satisfaction of the Psychological Needs of our Phase is the determining element of day-to-day motivation and optimal functioning.

Identifying the Base is important because, on the one hand, we "hear" better from our Base, and it is therefore the most important contact point or point to re-establish contact. Whilst on the other hand, de-motivation is a result of not getting the Base needs met.

However, it is not quite so simple! Satisfying Phase needs is motivating, yet if we neglect the Psychological Needs of the Base, this can be de-motivating, so we must take care to recognize all our psychological needs.

Example from Professional Life

Michel is head of purchasing in a service company. His Base is Thinker with an Imaginer phase. His boss knows him well and being familiar with PCM knows that he has to let Michel have the time and a quiet place in which to visualize the implementation of projects where he can work in peace and quiet without too many interruptions.

When the end of the year arrives, with all the reports to be given and for the supplier files to be wound up and paid off, Michel's boss drops by to give him clear and concise instructions. He then gives him space and lets him go to work. It has always worked very well like that.

But six months ago the company merged with an American company and the process of task verification has multiplied, and now any operation involving transfers of funds requires multiple entries into the data base using new software.

Lately Michel has become bad-tempered and very critical of the new process that he considers an "absurd and dangerous waste of time." He quibbles about the smallest delay and no longer lets even small errors of his colleagues get by without comment. He becomes extremely angry when his suppliers don't do exactly what he wants. He was once the exact opposite, calm and accommodating, and now he was becoming very controlling.

Michel's boss gives him more space and time. He nourishes his Phase need (solitude) and yet Michel remains aggressive and progressively more and more de-motivated and the source of stress for others.

We observe that Michel is displaying frustration from his Thinker Base by "over controlling" and being critical; attacking his company's methods. The new process recently implemented by the American management is frustrating the Psychological Needs of the Thinker base (recognition for work and need for structure). Even when his boss offers him what he usually needs (need of solitude of the Imaginer Phase), it is to no avail; he remains furious and becomes much less effective.

For Michel to get his smile back and for him to return to his usual competent self, his boss (or the management) must nourish Michel's need for work recognition and structure so he gets back to "functioning" normally.

Taibi Kahler explains it this way:
The needs of our Phase are the keys to current motivation;
The needs of the Base are essential to foster emotional functioning.
The satisfaction of these needs cannot be ignored. When needs are frustrated, the individual loses energy and motivation.

When colleagues are de-motivated, we can help by offering what is necessary to feed their Phase needs (*motivation*) and also to provide nourishment for their Base needs (*emotional balance*). Simply focusing on phase needs will not be enough when there is de-motivation.

> ## In Brief
>
> If I want others to listen to me, I will speak their Base language.
> If I want to invite motivation for others, I will offer their Phase Psychological Needs, and in order to avoid de-motivating them, I shall be careful not to deprive them from their Base Psychological Needs.

6. Driver Behaviors

A *Driver* is the first signal that we are experiencing stress and entering distress stress. Drivers take their name from the recognition that these behaviors appear to be "driven" from our unconscious; they are patterns of behaviors we have learned to use as a sort of "magical" protection, like a talisman.

> Before you continue reading, ask yourself the following questions:
> Have I ever been troubled because I had to say "No?"
> Have I ever been troubled when examining my work, because I found it flawed and thought that it could be improved?
> Have I ever said to myself, "You are alone and there is no one to help you" or "I'm the only person I can count on."
> Have I ever been irritated when I see that others are not doing a good job?
> Have I ever been irritated when someone asks me for help?
> Have I ever felt as though my head was in a thick fog and that I just couldn't understand what someone was explaining to me or asking me?

"When I experience one of these situations it's more than I can handle, I have to…" You could finish the sentence couldn't you? From the above we are about to describe a miscommunication behavior directly linked to stress.

- Under stress, I can no longer think straight: I perceive an *altered reality*.
- Under stress, my feelings are dictated by this altered reality and seem to turn into *"parasite emotions"* draining me of my normal coping strategies.
- Under stress, I act under the influence of the two aforementioned phenomena. I, then, make inappropriate decisions, and I adopt inappropriate behavior (ineffective, even negative). We call these behaviors 'Driver Behaviors'.

6.1 Definition of *Driver* Behaviors

Drivers are subtle behaviors, acquired in childhood, which helped us to avoid uncomfortable feelings. They seemed to act like a lucky charm, "I will be OK just so long as I ...."

Seemingly effective in the past, we revert to these behaviors today when we experience environmental pressures drawing us into stress. However, although we have used these patterned coping strategies for many years, they really don't work and even worse can act to make us less-resistant to stress.

> **Driver behaviors are:**
> **Behaviors** that seem to offer protection from a potentially uncomfortable emotion.
> **Subtle** because we seldom perceive our driven behavior;
> **Learned, acquired and there is some evidence to say are innate and therefore, linked to our temperament**. Driver behaviors are integrated as unconsciously available and instinctive. Entering into these behavioral patterns is from our unconscious and is outside of awareness.

When we enter into *Driver* behavior, a part of the energy that we could use to think clearly is used to act out old internal recordings (little voices) that say to us or that we may suggest to others: "You only have value if ..."

Taibi Kahler identified one *Driver* specific to each Personality Type:

Thinker:	**Be Perfect** (for others)
Words:	Over-explains & unnecessary qualifications
Tones:	Measured
Gestures:	Punctuating with fingers or hand

Postures:	Measured; robotic
Facial Expressions:	Strained
Overall Behavior:	Over-thinks for others; reverse delegation of tasks, i.e. takes delegated work back
Examples:	

> "So there are in fact, six *Driver* behaviors, that is to say, repetitive behavioral patterns, well to me personally, six we use in PCM so to speak…"

"Well, what I intended to suggest, or that is to say, what I will propose as a solution, or at least as a temporary partial solving of the problem …"

Harmonizer:	**Please** (others)
Words:	Maybe; Kinda; You know …
Tones:	May be a little whining; pitch rises at the end of the sentence (turning a statement into a question)
Gestures:	Head nodding, chin tucked in; open handed (arms forward palms up)
Postures:	Shoulders in (rounded) Head and often body leaning towards the other
Facial Expression:	Smiling; raised eyebrows; timid; looking up from under the eyebrows
Overall Behavior:	Over-adapts to others, becomes indecisive

Examples:
"If you like, maybe I could clarify *drivers* for you."
"Oh I don't mind what we do tonight, you say."

Rebel:	**Try Hard** (for others)
Words:	I can't; ah, um; I don't know; I'll try; (asking indirectly for things)
Tones:	Strained and pressured
Gestures:	Helpless
Postures:	Leans forward; bent as if carrying a weight & with head up
Facial Expressions:	Struggling, wrinkled as if straining to remember or do something
Overall Behavior:	Invites others to think for them, delegates inappropriately and/or without direction
Examples:	

"Uh... er... how can I explain it...er...a *driver*, it's uh..."
"Um, I'll try to get the file of, oh what's his name?"

Imaginer:	**Be Strong** (for others)
Words:	"It came to me"; "It occurred to me"
Tones:	Monotonic
Gestures:	None
Postures:	Rigid; frozen
Facial Expressions:	Molded; cold; expressionless

Overall Behavior:	Withdraws inside; appears to "spin wheels"
Examples:	

"The image of a *driver* comes to me" (rather than "I am thinking of a driver").
"It occurs to me that this is best done alone." (Rather than, "I think")
"A thought just crossed my mind."

Persister:	**Be Perfect** (for me)
Words:	Uses big important-sounding words & over qualifications; Over details; Over questions
Tones:	Precise
Gestures:	Calculated
Postures:	Rigid; stiff; aloof
Facial Expressions:	Head tilted slightly upwards with slightly piercing eyes
Overall Behavior:	Focuses on what is wrong rather than what is right; expects others to be perfect
Examples:	

"Will you explain more clearly and precisely what you want to know about *drivers*?"
"This report has several spelling and grammatical errors in it. Don't you have a spell checker on your computer?"

Promoter:	**Be Strong** (for me)
Words:	"What makes you think.." "How did he make you feel?" (Uses you when means I)

Tones:	Meant to impress
Gestures:	Exaggerated
Postures:	Imposing
Facial Expressions:	Confident; unblinking
Overall Behavior:	Expects others to fend for themselves.
Examples:	

"Listen, get a grip! If you don't understand *Drivers,* do what I do, find out yourself"

"You can't make an omelet without breaking eggs!"

"If you can't take the heat, get out of the kitchen!"

7. Failure Patterns

Each Personality Type has a set of restricting and destructive beliefs that, under stress, can lead us to sabotage ourselves. The repetition of these beliefs and associated behaviors act like self-fulfilling prophesies, and each time we repeat the behaviors and achieve the same results, we confirm the belief system. These scripts (beliefs) are at times identifiable in our speech patterns.

> ### DEFINITION OF THE FAILURE PATTERN
>
> A Failure Pattern is a predictable, repetitive, and unconscious mental pattern that can lead to personal and/or professional failure.
> The script is driven under the influence of a *Driver*. We know from research that behavior that repeats itself reinforces itself. Given that *drivers* are behaviors that we developed in childhood, to attract conditional attention from the important people in our environment, we have been unconsciously repeating these patterns for a lifetime, and we continue to use them repetitively in our daily lives.
> These repetitions of behaviors, based upon unconscious beliefs, then interfere with our thinking, and this becomes apparent through our sentence patterns. These patterns can manifest themselves hundreds of times a day, and unless we notice them and act to interrupt this process, we may well go deeper into our failure mechanism and in so doing reinforce it.

7.1 "Until…" (Thinker or Persister Types)

Belief: "I can't enjoy myself until I have finished what I have to do perfectly …"

Speech Patterns: Lots of parentheses to explain the words used, as if the person was thinking: "Until I've cleared up and explained everything, I can't finish my sentence"; "It's essential (I mean important) to finish (rather, complete) this explanation (I mean presentation) with an example …"

Observable Behavior: Tendency to put off moments of relaxation, pleasure and intimacy in favor of completing the task.

7.2 "After…" (Harmonizer Type)

Belief: "Everything's going well for the time being, but it's too good to last."

Speech Patterns: People who show this pattern will point out things that are going well (start with a positive) then expresses concern about the future with a "but" (end on a negative): "I'm so glad I joined this team, but I wish I had come here sooner, life is so short?"

Observable Behavior: Tends to worry about the future seeming to believe that as things are going well now, it cannot last. Demonstrates anxiety by anticipating the arrival of a negative event. Either the person does nothing to avoid it or unintentionally provokes it by trying to please everybody at all costs.

7.3 "Always..." (Rebel or Promoter Types)

Belief: "Well if that's what you want to do, you can spend the rest of your life doing it." "You've made your bed, now you must lay in it."

Speech Patterns: Suggests alternatives that are contradictory or "absurd," often to justify inaction or a bad choice: "Yeah I suppose ... but if I show you the Power Point as I had planned, we won't have time to finish, but if I don't show it to you, you'll be frustrated ..."

Observable Behavior: Makes a decision painfully then questions it (Rebel). Hesitates to come to terms with the problem to escape frustration (Promoter).

7.4 "Never..." (Imaginer Type)

Belief: "I never seem to get what I most desire ..."

Speech Patterns: Tends to make sentences with no beginning or end, jumping from one subject to another and going off in tangents. "For example ...

in the presentation there was the idea that … I could suggest … in the end there is …"

Observable Behavior: Noticeable loss of energy. Becomes "invisible." Doesn't finish what is begun, and sometimes doesn't begin anything, saying that it won't work anyway.

There are two patterns that are formed by a combination of Base and Phase types. These process scripts are not seen in Base types.

7.5 "Almost…" 1 (Combination of Harmonizer and Rebel Base and Phase)

Belief: "I almost manage to do it, but just not quite. If only there hadn't been that *little glitch*."

Speech Patterns: "I almost finished that book and then I lost it." "That was a great book, but what was the last chapter all about?"

"I prepared some really visual aids and put them in my car the night before, but the next morning without thinking, I took my wife's car."

Observable Behavior: Fails with success within sight (often the result of invisible or unconscious self-sabotage).

7.3 "Almost…" 2 (Combination of Harmonizer and Thinker or Harmonizer and Persister Types)

Belief: "I almost make it and then discover an even bigger task to achieve." "Is this all there is?"

Speech Patterns: Has problems accepting the value of the success of a project important to him/her. "Of course we succeeded … I think we were lucky … That shows that the objectives were probably not ambitious enough." "I understand the meaning of PCM; I hope I will remember to use what I know tomorrow."

Observable Behavior: Deprecates success. Has everything to be happy, but isn't. Constantly looking for new goals. Finishes but quickly goes on to another challenge.

8. Failure Mechanisms

Every Personality Type has a specific way of going deeper into distress, through displays of negativity and hostility expressed toward others and themselves.

Failure mechanisms are unconscious yet predictable and observable behaviors. They result from our search to satisfy our Psychological Needs in a negative way because we unconsciously believe we cannot get these needs met positively and because we have drained our reserves of psychological energy.

8.1 Over-Controlling

This is typical behavior of the *Thinker type* under stress. People in a Thinker Phase show a tendency to impose their methods because they think the others are stupid.

8.2 Crusading

This is typical behavior of the *Persister Type* under stress. People in a Persister Phase show a tendency to impose their convictions and to go on "crusades" against projects or people because they believe that they are not worthy of confidence.

8.3 Blaming

This is typical behavior of the *Rebel Type* under stress. People in a Rebel Phase show a tendency to blame others for their mistakes, because they assume that anything bad that happens is the fault of others. ("If it weren't for John being late, I would have achieved my deadline. It's not my fault.")

8.4 Doing Nothing (Passive Inactivity)

This is typical behavior of the *Imaginer Type* under stress. People in an Imaginer Phase show a tendency to wait, doing and saying nothing, and hope the cause of the stress will disappear. They seem to think that by not taking action, the problems will vanish.

8.5 Making Mistakes

This is typical behavior of the *Harmonizer Type* under stress. People in a Harmonizer phase show tendency to let themselves become overwhelmed by their emotions. They fluster and make silly mistakes, seemingly losing control of their actions and words thinking that whatever they do, others will no longer like them.

8.6 Manipulation

This is typical behavior of the *Promoter Type* under stress. People in the Promoter Phase show a tendency to manipulate others by attempting to humiliate them or "push" them to error telling themselves, "It's not my problem; they are hurting themselves."

CHAPTER 5

FAQs about The Process Communication Model

> How do you quantify your model? Are there many percentages in the documents?
> What method was used to define the concepts?

Taibi Kahler is first of all a clinical psychologist. He works from catalogued and quantified observations. His model is built on a hypothesis based on observation of thousands of behaviors and confirmed with a statistical and clinical approach. The details of his studies and methods are available at www.kahlercommunications.com.

8.7 Are the Forty-Five Personality Pattern Inventory Questions Enough to Determine a Personality Structure?

The Personal Pattern Inventory questionnaire is computer analyzed and cross-checked numerous times. Each statement includes six items, five of which can be chosen by the participants.

There is also a psychotherapeutic questionnaire: the TASP.

8.8 Don't You Find It Dangerous to Use Words Like "Rebel," "Persister" etc.?

I believe in the complexity of human nature, and I feel that putting people in "pigeon holes" and labelling them is not at all helpful.

There is always a danger when working with typologies for individual Personality types and attributing qualities to them that we seem to reduce human experience to over simplistic descriptions. Talking about people as if they are just "Types" is rather demeaning. On the other hand, shortcuts or professional jargon has a use in offering a means to quickly transfer a large amount of complex information. In any event, it is human nature that we form an opinion or image of another without the aid of a profile. We may even attribute others with all kinds of traits without our conscious knowledge. It seems to be a natural and regrettable tendency to judge our neighbors.

What is worse is that we tend to use negative reference points as opposed to positive, as for example, to say of a friend or colleague, *"He's a little bossy."* rather than *"He likes to give guidance."*

PCM seeks to question what lies behind the image that we paint of others (what they most often show us).

In addition, in PCM, we identify a combination of six Personality Types making a possible combined total of 720 possible combinations of basic traits; so the Model demonstrates that even though we have some characteristics in common, each of us is unique, be it by education, by personal history, career and so on. With the second order of complexity of PCM, adding the Base and Phase combinations, we see a total of 4320 possibilities.

8.9 Concretely, What Is It for?

PCM is first and foremost a communication tool.

The idea is simple. In a few seconds, we can determine how to interact with others so as to create an exchange based upon the principles of win-win. We therefore, reduce negative competitiveness and thus save precious time and energy thanks to communication that works.

8.10 I'm Not Going to Think about Which Channel to Use Every Time That I Speak! One's Nature Always Quickly Resurfaces!

It is exactly because old behavior is not easily eradicated that we can concentrate our effort on how best to transfer our message before we begin our exchange: in this way we can both utilize our natural resources more effectively and quickly.

Our "natural" behavior can be changed with time, through practice, until the new behavior becomes natural. If we give ourselves permission to develop new skills through training and coaching, we enable ourselves to modify behavior that goes back almost to our date of birth.

There was a time in our lives when it was natural to crawl upon our hands and knees …

8.11 I'm a Little Concerned about the Potential for Manipulation in the Use of the Model.

We quickly become aware when a person tries to manipulate us especially if that person is "pretending to communicate" on our preferred Channel. When communication is not authentic, it is a maneuver or a "procedure" rather than a *Process*. By using the process and not a procedure, communication between individuals flows naturally. Using PCM we simply say what we have to say, in a way the other can more easily hear. In this way we take responsibility for our part in the communication and are still being authentic as we are simply using a different part of our personality from which to begin the interaction.

We can usually spot the difference between flattery and compliment. The first makes one feel good while the impact lasts longer with the second and at times, we may even find that flattery is annoying.

If we are not sincere in our relationships with others and we use manipulative "tricks," we will not be effective. The key to being effective with PCM then is a sincere intention to communicate effectively rather than to manipulate or to gain an advantage over others.

8.12   I Don't Think I Can Use the Style of a Personality Type That's Foreign to Me. It Wouldn't Be Me.

Process consists of using resources we already have available to us and to develop them so that we do experience "being ourselves" when we use a flexible communication style.

We all have the six floors of the personality condominium available to us. Some of the floors require reactivation through training and practice so we teach ourselves how to use them, but they are there and so are the real you.

Our Rebel side is different from that of someone else, as is our Harmonizer and so on. It is not a question of mechanically repeating the behaviors described in this book; that would be over-simplistic.

On the contrary, we can use what we are deep down inside, and this is being authentic and about valuing others enough to be willing to invest energy in meeting them in a more respectful and effective way. Remember, "If you want them to hear what you say, talk their language."

Appendix

1. Process Communication Model: Chronology

Taibi Kahler validates the material in 1975:

The **six personality types:** Consistent clusters of specific characteristics, shared by all human beings but in varying degrees according to individuals – 720 possible combinations of personality structure.

The **Base** of the structure: The dominant Personality Type of the individual.

The Existential Question: The reason we develop certain skills rather than others, and what constitutes for us the *sine qua non* condition for emotional well-being.

The four myths: Beliefs according to which we will emotionally depend on others or they on us.

The **Channels and Perceptions of communication:** Specifically how to address each Personality Type in order to be heard and understood.

The **Driver behaviors** (also known as "little voices"): Key discovery of Taibi Kahler, behavior under light stress, warning signals of the potential of sliding deeper into stress if not dealt with in time.

The **Failure Patterns**: Negative beliefs about ourselves, others and life, displayed in an individual's speech patterns;

The **failure mechanisms**: Behaviors of an unconscious origin which aim at meeting the individual's Psychological Needs negatively.

However, the need is only moderately met: studies made to correlate the questionnaire and typologies show a little more than a 65% correlation. That's good but it could be better.

His original hypothesis was that an individual will, under scripted stress (repeated and unconscious), display stress behavior of his Base (dominant type), with a 65% correlation; later, he returned to the data of the studies that, luckily, his mother had not thrown out!

He correlated these data starting from a new principle: The most frequent stress behaviors for an individual correspond to the frustration of a precise Psychological Need that is not necessarily that of the Base.

By comparing the data and the hypothesis he was seeking to prove, Kahler discovered that there were still points in his study to re-examine. He then discovered that for over 70% of the population, a second Personality Type influenced an individual's behavior. He then called this the *Phase Type*.

From this new given, he obtained a statistical correlation of 96%. Success!

Taibi Kahler then made his most important discovery: *Phase change*.

This discovery enabled him to validate an essential component of personality Phase Types: *problematic of Phase*. They are caused by an emotion or behavior specific to each Phase. They are at the origin of Phase change when the emotion or behavior that results is not dealt with spontaneously and genuinely.

In 1977, Taibi Kahler received the Eric Berne[1] Memorial Scientific Award from the Eric Berne Foundation for his work on miniscripts. This prize rewards discoveries that contribute to the significant advancements in Transactional Analysis.

2. Process Communication Model in France

In 1987 the psychologist, Gérard Collignon encountered Taibi Kahler and his therapy model, *Process Therapy*®. The two men struck up a friendship, and Collignon accepted Kahler's offer to develop the Process Communication Model in France.

To start, together with a group of colleagues, he launched the project to which he would quickly become very attached: the creation in 1987 of Kahler Communication France, which today has a staff of eight (four consultants and four pedagogical assistants) and a network of over 1700 certified by Master Trainers.

The office's first mission was to disseminate and protect PCM in France. The second was for KCF to train and certify professionals in the fields of training, coaching, therapy and more recently, recruitment in the Process Communication Model. It was also a consulting and training office in the classic sense.

Gérard Collignon's book *Comment leur dire ?... la Process Communication*[2] (How to say it?...Process Communication), has 80,000 copies printed to date and has contributed to the increased awareness of the model in France and Europe.

A new work written in collaboration with Pascal Legrand, associate consultant at KCF, was published in 2006 on the subject of coaching with the Process Communication Model[3]: "Understand to be Understood".

---

[1] This prize rewards discoveries that significantly advance the work of Dr. Berne in Transactional analysis

[2] Published in 1997 by Editions Dunod.

[3] Legrand P, Collignon G., *Coacher avec la Process Communication*, Dunod, 2006.

In the beginning, Collignon's ambition was to develop the Model in Europe. In 2000, in the wake of his successes, he offered to his associate at the time, Bruno Dusollier, the possibility to take over and create a new structure: Kahler Communication Europe, which continued the work of development and protection of the Model outside France. In 2009, Kahler Communication France bought back Kahler Communication Europe, now managed by Cyril Collignon

Under the auspices of Cyril, the Process Communication Model is now present all over Europe.

In 2011, Kahler Communication France bought the PCM rights for Africa and created Kahler Communication Africa.

In 2014, Gérard and Cyril Collignon and their team bought Kahler Communications Inc., the IP owner of Process Communication Model all over the world. Cyril is now President of Kahler Communications, Inc.

3. The miniscript
by Taibi Kahler
(addendum to the article of 1974)

I am grateful to the editorial board of TAJnet for this opportunity to revisit the original miniscript article and to update the applications and research done over the last twenty-eight years on the concept, and its offspring's, the Process Communication Model and Process Therapy®.

In 1972 I conducted a research project correlating drivers, ego states, psychological needs, life positions, rackets, script injunctions, scripts, roles, games, and myths. I administered the Kahler Transactional Analysis Script Checklist, which I had created for my dissertation to 1,200 people. With completed responses by 982, six of the ten Drivers (five from Child and five from the Parent) were selected as the most experienced: Please you, Try hard for you, Be strong for you, Be perfect for you, Be strong for you, Be perfect for you, Be strong for me, and Be perfect for me. Although this study did not demonstrate significant correlations between these six major groupings of driver (types) and expected item responses, there were significant correlations among non-driver related item responses constituting a natural loading on six clusters. For example, there was a strong correlation between and among, -CP, frustration, NIGYSOB, I'm OK - You're Not OK, Don't have fun, and the Until script. The mutually exclusive and significant factor loadings strongly suggested that six patterns were representing at least 95% of the negative behaviors, as identified by these T.A. terms. I had shared many of these correlations with a good friend and colleague, Dr. Paul Ware, who had read Shapiro's work and later postulated six adaptations. We both seemed to be on the same track, from differing directions.

I started teaching and writing about the six patterns and their correlations, calling them Overreactors, Workaholics, Doubters, Manipulators, Disapprovers, and Daydreamers, adding a seventh to identify some of the clinically unaccounted for population, and called this adaptation Cyclers.

About 1975, I began to travel and lecture a great deal, and slowly shifted away from clinical presentations to personal awareness and growth seminars, and then to business application conferences. With my role at NASA in 1978 in the selection and placement of the astronauts, came an obvious need for more efficient ways of interviewing hundreds of candidates.

The timing was perfect. Although I had not focused any more on clinical or miniscript applications, I had looked and thought a great deal about the positive behavior patterns of these primary six adaptations, and I began calling them Personality Types. It was time for more research.

For several years, I had been looking at personality structure as a layering of these six (positive) Personality types. I trained a group of Parent Educators in Florida over a period of twenty years. They in turn taught about ten thousand parents (an average of 500 parents of two through five-year olds in ten Lab Schools each year) how to assess personality structure, connect with their children, motivate them, and deal with their negative behaviors. We hypothesized that this ordering of these six Personality Types within an individual was mostly "set" by age seven. Subsequent test-retest research has substantiated that personality structure remains consistent over time.

In about 1978 I made perhaps the most important theoretical discovery of my life, including the miniscript. I called it "phases". I was searching for a key to unlock such questions as:
- Why people were motivated by different psychological needs at different times in their lives?
- Why a person's primary driver never changes even though he or she might have a negative miniscript sequence that will correlate to a positive personality type other than the one associated with this primary driver?
- Why people will or can have a different predominant script at different times of their lives?

- Why people can demonstrate not just one, but two negative miniscripts?

In order to answer these questions I began another study, finished in 1982, that included a research a paper and pencil inventory, and expanded the questions to connect Personality Types with character traits, environmental preferences and management styles. It also tested for phases, the emergence of a foreground personality type that determines, to some extent, what our new Psychological Needs will be, and what the new negative miniscript will be.

This research also tested for what had been observed in the perceptions of each of the six Personality Types. This was a consistent and logical outgrowth from Paul Ware's model of expanding Berne's feeling, thinking and behaving designations. I renamed "feelings" to "emotions". I observed the singularity "thoughts" to be a mixture of thoughts and opinion). And I observed "behaving" divided into action, reaction, and inaction. Results indeed indicated significant correlations between Reactors and emotions, Workaholics and thoughts, Persisters and opinions, Promoters and actions, Rebels and reactions, and Dreamers and inactions.

Three "experts" in assessing these six Personality Types independently interviewed 100 people. All six Personality types were represented in the sample. All three judges agreed on 97 assessments, yielding an interjudge reliability significant at >.001.

These same experts were to determine phase. Using again Kendall's coefficient of concordance, W, and testing this significance with the critical values of chi-square, interjudge reliability was again significant at >.001.

An additional number of people were assessed and selected by the judges independently so that a minimum number of 30 persons were available for each classification of Personality Type, yielding a total sample of 180 identified "assessed" people.

Two hundred and thirteen items including extractions from the original study item pool were administered to 112 randomly selected subjects. Analysis of this data indicated once again a natural loading on six criteria - - the six Personality Types.

Two hundred and four of these items were administered to the 180 identified Personality Types. Only items with a correlation of greater than .60 (significant at >.01) were accepted for inclusion in the final Personality Pattern Inventory (PPI).

I was elated not only with the results of the research, but with using it to reinterpret the 1972 research findings.

To illustrate with a typical example:
- *Promoter*: "Be strong for me!"
- *Dreamer*: "Be strong!"
- *Persister*: "Be perfect for me!"
- *Rebel*: "Try hard!"
- *Harmonizer*: "Please you!"
- *Workaholic*: "Be perfect!"

In the original research, if a person had a primary Be perfect driver, it was hypothesized that he or she would then experience the following cluster of behaviors: -CP, Don't have fun, frustration, NIGYSOB, Until, I'm OK - You're Not OK, etc., as these all were highly correlative.

91

Yet to be realized was the most important human behavioral factor, phases. In the above example, if the person had "phased" and was currently in the second floor identified as "Please you", then even though his primary, that is, most used observable driver, was still "Be perfect", the actual negative miniscript behavior will start with "Please you" and contain such correlatives: "I'm Not OK - You're OK"; "-AC", "victim"; "Stupid" and "Kick Me"; confusion; "Don't feel" your anger; "Almost"; etc. With such concurrent and predicative validity results, we could conclude that when a person does not get his/her phase-psychological-needs met positively, they will attempt to get the very same needs met negatively by coping and defending with the negative miniscript pattern that correlates with that phase personality type.

Therefore, since each person's behavior can be observed, described, explained, categorized, and monitored second by second with this model, I liken personality structure to a six floor condominium, complete with an elevator. The order is determined by birth (probably the first floor) and by environment (probably floors two through six.) There are 720 unique combinations, and with the identification of the phase, this yields a total of 4,320 unique personality structures, each floor of which has "energy" that can be measured from 1 to 100%. In other words, one could interpret that there are millions of positive miniscripts.

Although originally I identified five drivers from the Parent (i.e., I'm OK - - You would be if...) and five from the Child (i.e., You're OK - - I would be if...), only six of these ten drivers significantly correlated with other six factor loadings: Please you, Try hard for you, Be strong for you, Be perfect for you, Be strong for me, and Be perfect for me. In other words, observation and research suggests that six [negative] miniscript sequences describe and encompass a significant percentage of the general population.

Another result of the second research endeavor was the production of a paper and pencil inventory that gives these business, personal, and clinical correlations in the forms of profile reports and seminars. More than 500,000 people have now been profiled, in more than 20 countries, in 10 different languages, complete with reliability and validity scales. 135 people have been certified in the U.S. and 170 internationally.

Although it is not my purpose here to give a treatise on Process Therapy, I would be remiss if I did not caution the reader on several points postulated in the original article. Most importantly, drivers should neither be confronted directly, nor should they be "eliminated." The phase driver starts a negative miniscript sequence that connects that driver and a decisional consequence at the script injunction level. Therefore, the driver functions as a defense mechanism and should be treated as such: (As I recall, Bob and Mary Goulding identified this correctly and offered this caveat) There are, however, preferred transactions and perceptions to use when you transact with a person in a driver. Furthermore, just providing "permissions" relating to drivers or stoppers (functional script injunctions) is not likely to be profitable.

For those who would like an annotated research, including ten dissertations, and a presentation list or an overview of Process Therapy, including negative miniscript sequences, please e-mail me at kahlercom@aristotle.net. Please note that any teaching or training of non-clinical applications of the miniscript model (a.k.a. Process Communication Model) is copyrighted and requires certification by Kahler Communications, Inc. in the U.S., and Taibi Kahler Associates, Inc. in all other countries.

Taibi Kahler, January 1999.

4. INTERVIEW WITH TAIBI KAHLER

Taibi Kahler told us how he went from research into transactional analysis to the discovery of his Process Communication Model, both at the level of therapy (*Process Therapy*®) and personnel development (Process Co Management®).

The object of this interview, of 1st October, 2002, was to clarify the difference between the Process Therapy Model and the Process

Communication Model and at the same time how they were or were not linked to Transactional Analysis.

Dr. Kahler is Transactional Analysis the point of departure for your work?

I began to get involved in transactional analysis in 1969, and a short time after, I started to write articles about my observations, ideas and discoveries. That year, while engaged in the observation of my patients in a psychiatric hospital, I observed short and recurrent behavior patterns in the patients just prior to negative emotional outbursts or maladapted behavior. Using transactional analysis, I was able to name and catalogue these behaviors under stress as follows: CP-, AC-, or CV- (Critical Parent negative, Adapted Child negative, or Child Victim negative). I then understood that these negative ego states were nothing more than functional manifestations of projected or introjected injunctions.

What were your conclusions?

I concluded that these attitudes and behaviors, that in each case lasted only a few seconds and were followed by entry into CP-, AC- or CV-, had to be functional manifestations of a negative life script. After watching some forty hours of video tapes, I hypothesized that there were five negative life scripts using the behavioral diagnostic criteria of Dr. Eric Berne, the founder of Transactional Analysis: words, gestures, tone, posture, and facial expression.

Hadn't this been identified before?

No, not these short subtle and signaling occurrences of behavior identified elsewhere. I called them "*driver*" behaviors" using the expression of Freud who says we are "driven" toward neurotic behaviors.

What did you do with this important discovery?

Being mostly research-oriented, I set up, for my doctorate, a checklist of scripts that I administered to 1,200 people. My hypothesis at that time was that there were five *drivers* and that each one could be projected or introjected. I concluded that there could be up to thirty combinations of *drivers*-discreet interrupters (the name I, at that time, gave to injunctions).

Did you confirm your hypothesis?

Not completely. I expected to find significant correlation with other variables taken from Transactional Analysis. For example, I expected that a *driver* "Please others" would correlate in a significant way with the observation of an individual in the criteria groups:

AC (Adapted Child);
Negative Life Position "You're more valuable than me";
Under stress: Role of the victim;
Psychological Games: "Kick me in the butt!" and "I'm so stupid";
Injunctions: "Don't feel what you feel!" and "Don't grow up!";
Rackets of sadness and being unloved.

And among the concepts that I then developed I expected to find two of the four myths I had identified:

"I can make you feel good" and "You can make me feel bad";
The script "After";
The need for recognition as a person and sensorial needs.

As of 1972 I had gathered data on more than 982 subjects, and I had set up appropriate verification tests.

You seem dissatisfied with what followed.

I was both satisfied and dissatisfied with these results. Whatever the nature of the discovery I had made, it was clear that there were six unique patterns (*factor-loading*), but not the thirty I had imagined. Each of these mutually exclusive patterns suggested strongly that six of them concerned at least 95% of the negative behaviors of the general population as identified in the terms of transactional analysis. The *drivers* identified for each sequence of personality characteristics did present a significant correlation with a given failure script; however, only 65% to 70% were found in the complete chain of observation that I had previously described, for example the Reactor (now Harmonizer) Type.

That wasn't so bad!

Not enough to satisfy me. This led me to several conclusions:

The *driver* can generate a life script and not injunctions. It took me two years to discover that an individual's *driver* alters his speech patterns and engenders the negative script of that individual.

At the same time, I discovered that the injunctions, even though they don't engender the script, become more intense according to how frequently the individual activated them.

What I still couldn't explain was this: Even though there were probably only six *drivers*, it wasn't always the corresponding type of intervention that could end the negative sequence.

So you went back to the conclusions of Transactional Analysis?

I wrote Transactional Analysis articles on games, strokes, divorce, the education of young children, the behavioral categorization of each functional Ego States. Observing the Ego States in my way, I was able to demonstrate the existence of repeated sequential behaviors. I had begun to theorize on what I would call miniscripts beginning in 1971, and I used my research to consolidate my theory. But as I couldn't prove that there were, in fact, a finite (not infinite) number of possible miniscripts, I went back to my data that indicated a 65% to 70% correlation to be able to give at least a few examples of what I wanted to demonstrate in the *Journal of Transactional Analysis* in 1974.

You're speaking of your famous article on the miniscript?

Yes. I had presented lectures on the six sequences, but I didn't wish to publish my data that I considered incomplete and for which I hoped to arrive at higher correlation scores.

So when were the six types, Workaholic (now Thinker), Reactor (now Harmonizer), Rebel and the others born?

I shared with my colleagues the connections that I had made between the *drivers*, scripts, games, rackets, injunctions, myths and roles. I was concentrating at that time only on the aspects of negative behavior, and I had named the six miniscripts: Super-Reactors, Workaholics, Sceptics, Manipulators, Opposers, Day-dreamers; I even added a seventh, the Cycloids that seemed to be in the 5% that were missing from my initial analysis. I shared this correlation with my good friend the psychiatrist Paul Ware, who was immersed the work of Shapiro. Paul integrated into his work six clinical ntations" using my correlations and connecting them with classic lature of diagnostic psychiatry. He added to this approach visions - thought, emotions, and behavior - and set up a model for connection with patients that proved to be a powerful therapeutic tool. His process consisted of speaking to the patient using the preferred "door." He identified three doors: The entrance, the target door (that of development), and the trap door (the door to avoid).

In your work you often mention Paul Ware and his three doors to initiate contact with patients.

It is what later proved to be a powerful communication tool that I called perceptions. I, in fact, distinguished six doors and not three.

How is your Model different from Transactional Analysis?

In 1971 I wrote *Transactional Analysis Revisited* (published in 1978) in which I described how I used these miniscript models in clinical treatment. I called my model Process Therapy®. It was Transactional Analysis enriched with my discoveries: the miniscript, *driver* behavior, the four myths, negative Ego State sequences, the new life position "OK if…," speech patterns connected to the *driver* causing the scripts, and also my research linked to classic TA games, rackets, injunctions, roles, other life positions and even more. In 1977 I wrote a manual (published in 1978) called Process Therapy®, which focused on the seven miniscript sequences, my matrix, that of Paul Ware – thoughts/emotions/behaviors and positive transactions that I call channels – all this to create a model to use to invite patients out of stress.

What led you to continue your research, because you had already obtained significant results?

The same year, several important events happened in my life. For a long time I considered personality structure as a simple stacking of the six positive Personality Types in each individual. I observed not only maladapted behaviors under stress or in a clinical situation, but also I observed positive behavior. I had the vision of a house that would have six floors with an ensemble of positive characteristics on each floor. I constructed a hypothesis as to what these personality traits were for each Personality type. I called them: Reactor, Workaholic, Persister, Promoter, Dreamer and Rebel. I wished to work thereafter with neutral terms because I was no longer working from the clinical angle of Transactional Analysis scripts. The components that I found were:

Strengths of character;
Personality parts and their preferred Communication Channels;
Perceptions;
Preferred environment;
Management and interaction style;
Dress;
Facial expressions;
Preferred living environment (home and office);
Motivating psychological needs.

You considered your patients as being in good health.

I stopped considering only a single negative behavior schematic in clinical terms, but rather to consider the patient as a person whose personality structure was composed of six available types in a measurable, sequential order. While so doing, I asked myself question after question:

Why are people motivated by different psychological needs at different periods of their lives?

Why doesn't the primary *driver* ever change when the stress behavior sequence does seem to do so?

Why do some people show not one but two different stress sequences according to the intensity of the stress?

Why do others seem to change failure scripts during their lives?

As I was asking myself these questions, I remembered people I had encountered that had changed their lives, as if they had started down a new path after having learned from their sufferings. Their attitudes became different but their Base structure hadn't changed.

I still remember what appeared to me as the different "Phases" of my life.

Is that your discovery of "Phase Change"?

Absolutely! In exploring my memory looking for my own ce, I realized that each Phase of my life presented its own sequence as well as a different psychological need yet I had personality: It was, "Eureka!"

People begin with a miniscript that corresponds to the first floor (ground floor) of their six-story building. When the psychological needs of this floor of their building are not nourished positively, they display the miniscript of this type in order to nourish these same needs, even negatively.

And each miniscript has its own set of problematics, which is the key. When this is activated and then resolved, this key opens the door to change (what I call *Phase*) to the following personality, that is to say, the next floor.

This new Phase comes with a new miniscript, a new potential set of problematics, and a new psychological need as motivation in life.

And what happens with the rest, Base and other floors of the building when a Phase Change takes place?

The order of the floors of the building doesn't change, and the people present the same positive characteristics as before (That's what I thought then, which is not totally exact but close enough to my final discoveries).

Are you speaking of the research done for NASA?

Doing research was essential to demonstrate what my intuition was telling me. The timing was perfect. I had just been hired by Dr. Terry McGuire, the psychiatrist for NASA in charge of selection and management of crews, to help him select astronauts. Hundreds of the best of the best were candidates and NASA was looking for a more effective selection process than what they then had. They provided funding to continue my research in validation to be able to create a "pencil/paper" inventory so as to do a greater quantity of the work that we were doing, Dr. McGuire and I, in person-to-person interviews, using what I already called the Process Communication Model. This offered me the opportunity to broaden my research into non-clinical fields as well as test and validate my hypotheses. In 1978 I launched my company Taibi Kahler Associates, Inc. (TKA), invested, and registered the copyright for future articles, books, and manuals including the rights on the validation studies of the new inventory.

How did the research unfold?

The research began in earnest in 1979 and took several years. In 1982 it ended with exciting results. Starting from my 1972 research and in the light of my new hypotheses the data produced attained a significant level of >.01.

What was missing the first time?

The reason that I hadn't obtained such a high significant correlation the first time was that I hadn't included the factor of Phase change, which I hadn't yet hypothesized.

For example?

For example, only one person in three that displays a *driver* "please others" [that of the Reactor (now Harmonizer) Base] will show the miniscript sequence identified for the Reactor Type because he/she hasn't changed Phase. Two of three will have changed phase and will therefore show the miniscript sequence of the type that corresponds to the current phase. The inventory of ten components (Personality Pattern Inventory®) was validated both for a clinical and non-clinical approach. The validated research includes the confirmation of the existence of the six Personality Types, each with a measured sum of energy and in a sequential order of strong points, preferential environment, perception (the three of Berne and Ware are, in fact, six), Psychological Needs, management style, personality part, and Channel. The research made it possible to validate that the normal stress sequence of an individual corresponds to his/her Phase while the heavy stress sequence corresponds to the Base. I also validated that each type of personality has one or several Psychological Needs to nourish in priority; non-satisfaction leads the person to adopt a chain of behavior that tries to nourish this same need negatively, consciously or unconsciously. This made it possible to demonstrate how and why PCM made it possible to predict in an effective way the stress behaviors of astronauts and each of us

Today who can teach and offer your Model?

‑or that I created material applicable to certain environments, for the model, coaching, and therapy. Certification criteria ‑shed to authorize the use of this material by only trainers, ‑rapists certified by me or *master trainers* that I have empowered. Of course, anyone reading a work treating PCM (manager, parent, educator…) is "authorized" to use the material for themselves, but a non-certified person can in no case claim to know the model enough to teach it or use it in coaching or therapy, let alone to make money from it.

It's no longer Transactional Analysis …

I published fifteen articles in the *Transactional Analysis Journal* from 1972 to 1980. Later I chose to stop publishing in this journal because PCM was not TA (at their invitation I wrote an article in 1995 for TAJ for a special issue devoted to the laureates of the Berne Award in which I explained both PCM and Process Therapy). I used the principles of TA, but my work and research that came from it on the positive aspects of the personality are not in the domain of TA.

What is the place in clinical applications today?

The *Process Therapy Model* is today offered to help people in a therapy environment. Here again, I must insist on the fact that the application process and therapeutic use of the profile that goes with it must be done only by a TKA certified professional.

Selected Bibliography

Publications

BAILLY Béatrice, *Enseigner, une affaire de personnalité*, InterEditions, 1999. Process Communication and school age children. A work intended for professionals in education.

BRADLEY Dianne F., PAULEY, Judith A. AND PAULEY, Joseph F. *Effective Classroom Management: Six Keys to Success*. Nathan Publishing Company. Paris France. 1999. The authors offer unique and easy-to-implement strategies to manage classrooms and maximize student potential by designing management strategies and instruction that correspond to each child's personality type.

CHALUDE Michel, *Vous et votre projet*, InterEditions, 2001. An entertaining and clairvoyant book that presents the dynamics of leading a project in the light of Process Communication.

COLLIGNON Gérard, *Comment leur dire…: la Process Communication®*, InterEditions, 2002. Gérard Collignon's book is **the work** of reference on PCM. He presents the whole model in an amusing and structured way making it the perfect tool to continue one's development after a Process Communication Model seminar.

COLLIGNON Gérard, *Wie sag*. InterEditions. Paris, France. 1994.

COLLIGNON Gérard, LEGRAND Pascal, *Coacher avec la Process Communication®*, InterEditions, 2006. Over fifteen years of experience and practice in Process Communication coaching. This new work also presents the new concepts developed by Taibi Kahler such as problematics of personality types and their relationship with authentic emotions.

COLLIGNON Gérard, LEGRAND Pascal, *Understand To Be Understood*, Xlibris, 2016. In this book there is something for everyone. This book about coaching using PCM is overflowing with the complexity and at the same time the ordinariness of people in relationships.

DEHAIL Francine, *Le Management de la différence...avec la process Communication*. Editions de la Boheme. Saacy-sur-Marne, France. 1996.

DUSOLLIER Bruno, *Comprendre et pratiquer la Process Com®*, InterEditions, 2006. A practical work for coaches applying Process Comunication, My base, is Ok, I know; my phase, and I also know it better and better. But what happens with my base/phase association? Are there specific complementarities, or are there interactions that can accelerate the descent into stress?

FEUERSENGER Elisabeth, *Prozesskommunikation*. Weilheim Kahler Communication Germany, KCG. 2003.

FEUERSENGER Elisabeth and NAEF Andrea, *If you want them to listen, talk their language*. New Zealand Kahler Communications Oceania Ltd. 2011. This book explains the concepts of the Process Communication Model in a realistic and enjoyable way to enhance your ability to form and maintain relationships and skills for constructive communication and conflict resolution.

GILBERT Michael, *Communicating Effectively: Tools For Educational Leaders*. Scarecrow Education. 2004. This book provides a unique perspective for aspiring and practicing educational leaders to expand their problem-solving and conflict-resolution strategies.

KAHLER Taibi, *Communiquer, Motiver, Manager en Personne. InterEditions. Paris, France. 2003.

KAHLER Taibi, *Hetmysterie van het Management (in Dutch)*. Maklu. Antwerp, Belgium. 1999.

Manager

ᴋAHLER Taibi, *Manager en personne*, InterEditions, 2000. New version of Taibi ler's best seller, revised and expanded for France in an edition prefaced by ˙ Collignon. The only book written by Taibi Kahler available in French. ˙ining and educational approach to the Process Communication Model ⁀nagement situations.

Kahler Taibi, *The Mastery of Management (in English)*. Kahler Communications, Inc. Little Rock, AR. 1988, 2000. If you share a sleuth's love for a good mystery, and also believe that mismanagement is a crime, this book will be delightful, challenging, and stimulating reading.

Kahler Taibi. *The Mastery of Management (in Japanese)*. The English Agency (Japan) Ltd. Tokyo, Japan. 1993.

Kahler Taibi, *The Process Therapy Model (The Six Personality Types With Adaptations)*. Taibi Kahler Associates, Inc. Little Rock, AR, 2008.

Kahler Taibi, *The Process Therapy Model (The Six Personality Types With Adaptations – in German)*. Kahler Communication - KCG. Germany. 2008.

Lefeuvre Jérôme, *Découvrir la Process Communication*. InterEditions. Paris, France. 2007.

Lefeuvre Jérôme, *Pratiquer et s'entrainer à la Process Com en trente jours (exercices pratiques)*. Intended for those haying participated in a seminar or having discovered the model, a book with thirty days of exercises to become a confirmed "process commer!" to be published.

Pauley Judith A., Bradley Dianne F., and Pauley Joseph F., *Here's How To Reach Me: Matching Instruction to Personality Types in Your Classroom*. Paul H. Brookes Publishing Co., Baltimore, MD. 2002. Understand your students' personalities and you'll know the secret to communicating effectively with them!

Pauley Judith A. and Joseph F., *Communication: The Key to Effective Leadership*. ASQ Quality Press. 2009.

Pauley Judith A. and Joseph F., *Establishing a Culture of Patient Safety*. ASQ Quality Press. 2012.

Dissertations

APPOLD Barbara E., M.Ed., 2005, Central Michigan University. Dissertation, *A Case Study of the Impact Teachers with Awareness of the Process Communication Model on Student Achievement.*

> Found: 1) awareness of PCM was not sufficient to produce reliable, significant results in student academic growth scores, 2) teacher application of PCM may not have been fully implemented or be consistent, 3) longer and more extensive training in PCM, with support, review, and evaluation was needed.

BAILEY Rebecca Ed.D., 1998, University of Arkansas at Little Rock. Dissertation, *An Investigation of Personality Types of Adolescents Who Have Been Rated by Classroom Teachers to Exhibit Inattentive and/or Hyperactive-Impulse Behaviors.*

> Found statistically significant differences between student personality designations and the inattentive and hyperactive-impulse subscales. The combined findings suggest there were personality characteristics within a student's personality that would predispose him or her toward exhibiting what were perceived by teachers as inattentive and/or hyperactive-impulsive behaviors. Implications and recommendations were suggested for student assignment, for professional development of staff, and for related administrative considerations. The most compelling finding was that miscommunication between teachers and students due to a difference in personality type may be the reason many students are referred for and consequently labeled with Attention-Deficit Hyperactivity Disorder. This raises questions about the learning environment, the need to medicate students, and the utility of labels.

CARPENTER Craig, Ed.D., 1994, Arizona State University. Dissertation, *Depressed Children: Brief Intervention Strategies for Teachers.*

> Found PCM to be a valuable model for teaches in the understanding of and brief interventions with Reactor Personality Type depressed children.

DONLAN Ryan, Ed.D., 2009, Central Michigan University. Dissertation, *An*

Investigation of the Relationship between Michigan Charter School Leaders' Personality Strengths and the Schools' Performance Indicators Under Education Yes!.

Found that a statistically significant, moderate negative correlation existed between Workaholic strength of personality in school leaders and their schools' Overall School Performance Indicator scores in the accreditation system as reflected through Michigan's School Improvement Framework. Thus, leaders with stronger Workaholic strength of personality may adversely affect a school's school improvement efforts. Also, the study found that base personality types of charter school leaders were not substantially different than other educators found in Gilbert's (2005) research, yet phase personalities revealed a notable difference. Further, moderate, yet statistically significant negative correlations were found to exist between Workaholic strength of personality and three different strand areas of Michigan School Improvement - those of Teaching for Learning, Personnel and Professional Learning, and Data and Information Management. Yet, with respect to this finding, the research is not pointing to a direct correlate between a Workaholic strength of personality and that leader's adeptness with data; it is pointing to a correlation between Workaholic strength of personality and certain things that leaders do with the data, including but not limited to dialoguing about data, collaborating with others regarding data, engaging in conversation with other people about school-wide information, and creating a certain degree of safety in discussions concerning data.

EYERS CHRISTINA, ED.D.,2009, Central Michigan University. Dissertation, *Personality Patterns of NCAA Wrestlers and their Relationship to Disordered Eating: Implication for Educational Leaders.*

Found that the independent variables of NCAA Division level, weight category, personality strength, and current psychological need did not have a relationship with eating disorder risk. However, when accounting for the independent variables of NCAA Division level, weight category, and current psychological need, personality strength ($p < .05$) had a moderating effect on eating disorder risk. Furthermore, when controlling for the independent variables of weight category, personality strength, and current psychological need, NCAA

Division level indicated a mild trend toward significance (p < .1) with eating disorder risk. Due to the trend towards significance of personality strength with the relationship between NCAA Division level and eating disorder risk (p < .1), it was determined that personality strength had a moderating effect on NCAA Division level and eating disorder risk. Thought and belief oriented personality strengths represented 56.8% of the participants in this study.

FRANCISCO, MARK, ED.D., 2005, Central Michigan University. Dissertation, *An investigation of the relationship between administrator personality and teacher job satisfaction from a sample of Michigan k-12 public schools.*

Found that public school administrators who had experienced a phase change in their personality condominium were more likely to have happy staff members, likely enabling them to accept differences in personalities more readily. Antidotal but not empirically supported evidence suggested that divorced administrators may have more happy staff members, possibly due to their own phase shift as a result of their personal crisis. This was a surprise in the findings that has not yet been fully explored.

HALL GAVIN R., 1995, Leeds University, London, England. Dissertation, *The Process Communication Model of Humanistic Psychology as a Rehearsal Aid in the Creation of Character and Character Interaction.*

Found that the following elements of the PCM valuable to writers, directors, and actors: a knowledge of the psychological needs of personality type gives an actor a solid foundation of what drives the character; personality parts (a.k.a., ego states) creates a more subtle and interesting relationship between characters; channels of communication (a.k.a., transaction) enable actors to communicate the text in greater depth and understanding to the audience; a PCM textual analysis allows a director to come to a first rehearsal with a full picture of the world of the play, the elements of the characters, and the relationship to each other and the message of the play.

HAWKING Nancy, ED.D., 1995, University of Arkansas at Little Rock. Dissertation, *A Study of the Impact on Student Achievement by Teachers Training in Process Communication.*

Found that teachers trained in Process Communication positively affect student performance through understanding different student personality type needs and preferences.

JOHNSTON Richard, M.A., 1997, McGregor School of Antioch University. Thesis, *The Value of the Process Communication Mode to a Mediator.*

Found that the PCM model allowed the mediator to be in a better position to assess the people negotiating; helped the mediator to identify how each negotiator views their world, understand what preferences each has for interacting with their world, recognize each negotiator's probable distress levels, and motivate each negotiator to behave more in their non-distress way, thus helping to increase each participant's level of clear thinking and good engagement in [completing] the mediation process. The PCM also offers the mediator valuable information on what "not" to say or do, and then what and how to say the "best" thing to each negotiator. Furthermore the mediator can use this model to monitor himself/herself for insight into self behavior and a template for making self management decisions.

KAHLER Taibi, Ph.D., 1972, Purdue University. Dissertation, *Predicting Academic Underachievement in Ninth and Twelfth Grade Males with the Kahler Transactional Analysis Script Checklist. Dissertations Abstracts International-A*, 33(09), 4838 (University Microfilms No. AAT7306052)

Found correlations between the T.A. checklist items and underachievers, suggesting further research in comparing a "Stupid" criterion and underachieving.

MARTIN Sue, Ed.D., 2001, University of Arkansas at Little Rock. Dissertation, *A Study of the Behavior Causes of Miscommunication in Arkansas Elementary Public School Students.*

Found that there is a statistically significant difference in teachers reading and understanding their own personality profiles, and planning for student differences improved student behaviors.

MLINARCIK, John, Ph.D., 1990, The Fielding Institute. Dissertation, *Alcoholic Personality Types Revisited a la Kahler's Process Communication.*

Found that Reactive, Type II alcoholics had significantly lower mean Workaholic scores than the matched, nonalcoholic comparison subjects. Results support the movement favoring etiological theories that certain personality and psychological facts may lead to the development of Type II, "Process Reactive Alcoholism."

NASH Barbara, Ph.D., 1984, Western Michigan University. Dissertation, *Process Therapy: A Reliability and Validity Study.*

Found that Process Therapy could be a useful and practical model for diagnosis and treatment.

SHCOLNIK Bonnie, Ph.D., 1987, The Fielding Institute. Dissertation, *The Process Communication Model Concept of Developmental Processes: The Effects of Phase Development in Husbands on Marital Satisfaction of Wives.*

Found that PCM was a useful model for understanding how people might interact in a marital relationship: PCM can predict accurately that a certain personality type and phase individual would experience in a relationship with someone who is a different personality type or phase. Also results point out clearly that PCM is useful in predicting how people will communicate and whether or not specific psychological needs will be issues for them in a relationship.

THOMPSON Jon, Ed.D., 2006, Central Michigan University. Dissertation, *Adapting the Process Communication Model for Higher Education Writing.*

Found that teachers and students who have differing personality structures will have more miscommunication, and that the resulting negative coping strategies that will be used by both the teacher and student are predictable as a function of their personality typing in PCM.

WALLIN Mark, Ph.D., 1992, Northern Arizona University. Dissertation, *Making the Grade The Effects of Teacher Personality Types on Student Grading Practices.*

Found that a student's grade is significantly affected by the difference in personality structure between that of the teacher and that of the student.

Weisenbach Janice L., Ed.D., 2004, Central Michigan University. Dissertation, *An Investigation Of The Relationship Between Principal's Personality And A School's Organizational Climate In Lutheran Elementary Schools In Michigan.*

>Found that correlation test results between personality energy and Open climate produced an inverse correlation with Promoter energy. As the principal's Promoter energy level increased, the openness of the school decreased. School climate scores remained in the Open category; however, they were less open compared with schools where the principal did not have high Promoter energy.

TO KNOW MORE

Contact KCI

Kahler Communications, Inc.
1401 Malvern Ave., Ste. 140
Hot Springs, AR 71901
501-620-4744
www.kahlercomcommunications.com

KCI Copyrighted Elements

[Printed for legal reasons]

1. The six Personality Types: Workaholic (now called Thinker), Reactor (now called Harmonizer), Persister, Dreamer (now called Imaginer), Rebel, Promoter. Taibi Kahler, Ph.D., *Director*, Kahler Communications, Inc., Little Rock, Arkansas, 1988, 1992, 2000, 2004.

2. The personality structure is made up of the six Personality Types.

The personality building Taibi Kahler, Ph.D. *Process Communication Management Seminar*, Taibi Kahler Associates, Inc., Little Rock, Arkansas, October 1982, 1996.

3. Each Personality Type shows three character strengths: Workaholic (responsible, logical, organized); Harmonizer (compassionate, sensitive, warm); Persister (observant, dedicated, conscientious); Dreamer (imaginative, reflective, calm); Rebel (spontaneous, creative, playful); Promoter (adaptable, charming, resourceful). Taibi Kahler, Ph.D., *Manager*, Kahler Communications, Inc., Little Rock, Arkansas, 1988, 1992, 2000, 2004

4. These six Personality Types are found in each of us with a different sequence of strengths from the age of seven, and generally don't change. Stansbury, Pat, *Report of Adherence*, according to the observations on the same subject with the help of the Personal Pattern

Inventory that was taken twice. Kahler Communications, Inc., Little Rock, Arkansas, 1990.

5. Each Personality Type has his/her own personal management and relationship style; the Workaholic and Persister use the democratic style, the Reactor uses the democratic style, the Rebel uses the laissez-faire style, the Promoter uses and Dreamer accepts the autocratic style. Taibi Kahler, Ph.D., *Manager*, Kahler Communications, Inc., Little Rock, Arkansas, 1988, 1992, 2000, 2004.

6. The identified personality parts are: protector, sensor, comforter, director, computer, and emoter. Taibi Kahler, Ph.D. *Process Communication Management Seminar*, Taibi Kahler Associates, Inc., Little Rock, Arkansas, October 1982, 1996

7. Each Personality Type has a corresponding personality part: Workaholic, Persister and Dreamer use the computer part; Reactor uses the comforter part; the Rebel uses the emoter part; the Promoter uses the director. Taibi Kahler, Ph.D., *Process Communication Management Seminar*, Taibi Kahler Associates, Inc., Little Rock, Arkansas, October 1982, 1996.

8. Five channels are identified: interventive channel (1) makes the offer from the protector and is accepted by the sensor; directive channel (2) makes the offer from the director and is accepted by the computer; the requestive channel (3) makes the offer from the computer and is accepted by the computer; the nurturative channel (4) makes the offer from the comforter and is accepted by the emoter; the emotive channel (5) makes an offer from the emoter and is accepted by the emoter.

Taibi Kahler, Ph.D., *Process Communication Management Seminar*, Taibi Kahler Associates, Inc., Little Rock, Arkansas, October 1982, 1996.

9. Persister and Workaholic types use the requestive channel (3) together. Promoter transmits on the directive channel (2) towards the Dreamer; the Rebel uses the emotive channel (5) together; the Harmonizer uses the nurturative channel together and towards the rebel.

Taibi Kahler, Ph. D., *Process Communication Management Seminar*, Taibi Kahler Associates, Inc., Little Rock, Arkansas, October 1982, 1996.

10. The following perceptions correspond to the listed personality types:

Workaholic: thoughts

Persister : opinions

Harmonizer : emotions

Dreamer : inaction

Rebel : reactions ("I like..," "I don't like...")

Promoter: actions

Taibi Kahler, Ph.D., *Manager*, Kahler Communications, Inc., Little Rock, Arkansas, 1988, 1992, 2000, 2004.

11. Each Personality Type has a preferential environment, according to the following matrix: the vertical line is the goal axis; the horizontal is the relationship axis. The upper point is called internal motivation; the lower point is called external motivation. The point on the left is called engaged; the point on the right is called in retreat.

This forms the four quadrants. The upper left quadrant contains the Reactor type that prefers groups, the upper right quadrant contains the Persister and Workaholic types that prefer one-to-one relationships, the lower right quadrant contains the dreamer type that prefers to be alone, the lower left quadrant contains the rebel and promoter types that prefer to go from group to group or be on the edges of varied groups.

Taibi Kahler, Ph.D. *Process Communication Management Seminar*, Taibi Kahler Associates, Inc., Little Rock, Arkansas, October 1982, 1996.

12. Each Personality Type has received a recurrent theme (AKA "the existentialist question"):

Workaholic: "Am I competent?"

Persister: "Am I worthy of confidence?"

Promoter: "Am I alive?"

Dreamer: "Am I wanted?"

Rebel: "Am I acceptable?"

Harmonizer: "Am I likeable?"

Spencer/Shenk/Capers and Taibi Kahler Associates. *Process Communication Seminar*, Gardena, California, 1989 ; Taibi Kahler, Ph.D., Building Quality Teams, Kahler Communications, Inc., Little Rock, Arkansas. 1990, 1996.

13. Personality type phases and psychological needs:

Workaholic [phase]: needs recognition for work and structured time.

Persister [phase]: needs recognition for work and convictions.

Harmonizer [phase]: needs recognition of person, sensory satisfaction.

Rebel [phase]: needs contact.

Dreamer [phase]: needs solitude.

Promoter [phase]: needs excitement.

Taibi Kahler, Ph.D., *Manager*, Kahler Communication, Inc., Little Rock, Arkansas, 1988, 1992, 2000, 2004.

14. Three degrees of stress: First degree-the entry door; second degree-the basement; third degree-the cellar. Taibi Kahler, Ph.D. *Process Communication Management Seminar*, Taibi Kahler Associates, Inc., Little Rock, Arkansas, October 1982, 1996

15. Drivers are: "the observable behavior of negative miniscript sequences." Taibi Kahler discovered the five base *drivers*: "Please others," "Try hard," "Be perfect," "Be strong," "Hurry up," with which there are corresponding words, tone of voice, gestures, postures, and facial expressions. Taibi Kahler, Ph.D., with Hedges Capers, Div. M, LHD. "The Miniscript," *Transactional Analysis Journal*, 4:1, pp. 26-42, January 1974.

16. Each personality type has a primary *driver*: workaholic - be perfect (I have to be perfect for others); persister - be perfect (for me); harmonizer - please others; rebel - try hard (I must try hard for others); dreamer - be strong (I must be strong for others); promoter - be strong (for me). Taibi Kahler, Ph.D. *Process Communication Management Seminar*, Taibi Kahler Associates, Inc., Little Rock, Arkansas, October 1982, 1996.

17. A first degree of "mismanagement" behavior is associated with each type of personality *driver*:

Workaholic -"Be perfect": the manager does not delegate well;

Persister - " Be perfect" (for me): the manger focuses on what is not going well and is not good;

Harmonizer - "Please others": the manager is too attached to the well being of others and has problems taking decisions;

Rebel - "Try hard (I must try hard for others)": the manager has problems knowing what to do and delegates badly:

Dreamer - " Be strong (I must be strong for others)"; the manager waits for things to take care of themselves and does not take decisions;

Promoter - "Be strong (for me)": does not provide support ("figure it out for yourself").

Taibi Kahler, Ph.D., *Manager*, Kahler Communication, Inc., Little Rock, Arkansas, 1988, 1992, 2000, 2004.

18. At the second degree of stress each Personality Type displays a failure mechanism: the Workaholic over controls; the Persister imposes personal beliefs; the Reactor makes mistakes; the Rebel blames; the Dreamer waits passively; the Promoter manipulates. Taibi Kahler, Ph.D., *Manager*, Kahler Communication, Inc., Little Rock, Arkansas, 1988, 1992, 2000, 2004.

19. At the second degree of stress each Personality Type wears a mask: the Workaholic and the Persister wear an attacker's mask; the Harmonizer and the Dreamer wear the mask of a victim; the Rebel and the Promoter wear the mask of a blamer. The masks are identifiable with words, tone of voice, gestures, postures, and facial expressions.

Taibi Kahler, Ph.D. *Process Communication Management Seminar*, Taibi Kahler Associates, Inc., Little Rock, Arkansas, October 1982, 1996.

20. At the second degree of stress each personality type displays warning signals:

Workaholic: frustrated when others don't think logically, gets obsessed with time, money, order, cleanliness;

Persister: extremely sensitive to criticism, becomes suspicious and critical. Believes that only his/her opinions are right;

Harmonizer: no longer confident, laughs at him/herself inappropriately, invites criticism;

Rebel: appears negative, complains. Uses "yes but" with others, and blames others, events and situations;

Dreamer: withdraws into passiveness, no initiative, and projects are not finished;

Promoter: starts fights, ignores or breaks rules, and manipulates others.

Taibi Kahler, Ph.D. *Process Communication Management Seminar*, Taibi Kahler Associates, Inc., Little Rock, Arkansas, October 1982, 1996.

21. At the second degree of stress each personality type displays life position behavior:

Workaholic and Persister display; "I'm OK / You're not OK";

Harmonizer and Dreamer display: "I'm not OK / You're OK";

Rebel and Promoter display: "I'm OK / You're not OK."

Taibi Kahler, Ph.D. *Process Communication Management Seminar*, Taibi Kahler Associates, Inc., Little Rock, Arkansas, October 1982, 1996.

22. At the third degree of stress each personality type foresees a negative final benefit:

Workaholic: wants to exclude those that do not think clearly;

Persister: wants to exclude those that are not reliable;

Harmonizer: feels he/she will be excluded because "they no longer love me";

Rebel: reacts with: "If you reject me, I'll show you!"

Dreamer: waits to be told what to do and is surprised when excluded;

Promoter: wants to exclude those that can't take it.

23. When an individual displays a *driver*, the appropriate intervention model is the use of the channel and perception associated with the type revealed by the *driver*.

with " Be perfect (for you)" use the requestive channel and thought;

with " Be perfect (for me)", use the requestive channel and opinions;

with "Please others (for you)" use the nurturative channel and emotions;

with "Try hard (for you)" use the emotive channel and reactions [I like/I don't like];

with " Be strong (for you)" use the directive channel and inaction;

with " Be strong (for me)" use the directive channel and actions

Taibi Kahler, Ph.D., *The Advanced PCM Seminar*, Kahler Communications, Inc., Little Rock, Arkansas, 1997.

24. Each phase type of the Personality Type has potential problematics which determine whether an individual will or will not change phase in the course of a lifetime:

Workaholic: sorrow linked to loss;

Persister: fear;

Harmonizer: anger;

Rebel: responsibility;

Dreamer: autonomy;

Promoter: contacts.

Taibi Kahler, Ph.D., *The Advanced PCM Seminar*, Kahler Communications, Inc., Little Rock, Arkansas, 1997.

25. Each base Personality Type has a script with a failure sequence that is observable in speech patterns:

Workaholic and Persister: "Until";

Harmonizer: "After";

Rebel and Promoter: "Always";

Dreamer: "Never."

Certain combinations of Personality Types produce the scripts "Almost 1" and "Almost 2" Professional and Personal.

Taibi Kahler, Ph.D., *Process Communication Management Seminar*, Taibi Kahler Associates, Inc., Little Rock, Arkansas, October 1982 ; Taibi Kahler, Ph.D., *The Advanced PCM Seminar*, Kahler Communications, Inc., Little Rock, Arkansas, 1997.

26. The four myths are: "I have the power to make you feel good"; "I have the power to make you feel bad"; "I think that you have the power to make me feel good"; "I think you have the power to make me feel bad." Taibi Kahler, Ph.D., *Transactional Analysis Revisited*, Human Development Publications, Little Rock Arkansas, 1978.

27. PTM (*Process Therapy Model*) sets out the defense mechanisms of the first degree of each type:

Workaholic: rationalization;

Persister: projection;

Harmonizer: internalization;

Rebel: transfer;

Dreamer: depersonalization;

Promoter: charm.

Taibi Kahler, Ph.D., *Transactional Analysis Script Profile (Guide for the Therapist)*, Taibi Kahler Associates, Inc., Little Rock, Arkansas, 1997.

28. PTM (*Process Therapy Model*) presents the rackets, games and injunctions for each Personality Type, based on research and produced from a computer generated profile inventory. Taibi Kahler Ph.D., *The Transactional Analysis Script Profile*, Taibi Kahler Associates, Inc., Little Rock, Arkansas, 1997.

© March 1, 2006, Taibi Kahler, Ph.D.

Made in the USA
Middletown, DE
30 June 2019